LEARNING, to BELONG

BE at home in GOD'S WORLD

A 28-Day Devotional Journey

Book One of the Learning to Live Series

John van de Laar

In memory of my father, Ken van de Laar

Sacredise Publishing
Cape Town

SACREDISE PUBLISHING
P.O. Box 27212, Rhine Road
Cape Town, 8050
South Africa
http://sacredise.com

Unless otherwise indicated, all Scripture quotations are taken from the HOLY BIBLE, NEW LIVING TRANSLATION, copyright © 1996. Used by permission of Tyndale House Publishers, Inc., Wheaton, Illinois 60189. All rights reserved.
CEB refers to the COMMON ENGLISH BIBLE, copyright © 2011. All rights reserved. For more information see
http://www.commonenglishbible.com

Cover design by John van de Laar. Cover image from Shutterstock.com

ISBN 978-1481010061

OtheR BOOKS BY JOhn Van de LaaR

THE HOUR THAT CHANGES EVERYTHING – How worship forms us into the people God wants us to be

FOOD FOR THE ROAD – Life Lessons from the Lord's Table

contents

Learning to Live

*All of us are looking with unveiled faces at the glory of the Lord
as if we were looking in a mirror. We are being transformed into
that same image from one degree of glory to the next degree of
glory. This comes from the Lord, who is the Spirit.*
– 2 Corinthians 3:18 CEB

*All our life, so far as it has definite form, is but a mass
of habits. – William James*

Everyone worships something. Human beings are hard-wired to build our lives around some object, goal, person or belief system that gives us meaning, and that, we believe, will lead us to a good life[1]. Whatever provides us with this sense of meaning, becomes the object of our worship. And, whatever we worship, shapes who we are, how we spend our money, how we treat other people, what we drive and wear, and how we decide between right and wrong. Our worship defines our lives.

---

[1] For the inspiration for these thoughts, I am indebted to James K. A. Smith's book, *Desiring the Kingdom – Worship, Worldview and Cultural Formation,* (Grand Rapids, Baker Academic, 2009).

During his ministry, Jesus made the startling claim that he came to give "abundant" life.[2] Through the centuries, a few brave women and men have risked everything on this promise. Their testimony is remarkably consistent that a truly abundant life is found when we build our lives on God's Reign, just as Jesus did.

However, following Jesus does not come naturally to us. It must be learned through a constant process of visioning, listening, communicating and practising. This is why the act of worship is so important. Our worship services are classrooms in which we receive a vision of God's Reign, in which we learn the words, actions and attitudes of Christ, and in which we develop the habits that shape our lives according to Jesus' way. When we allow the habits of our worship to become the habits of our lives, we become true followers of Christ, and we enter into the abundant life that he promised.

This is the work of this *Learning to Live* series of books. Each volume will focus on one specific practice of worship, exploring what it means and how it teaches us to live well. The content is devotional, engaging both heart and mind, and includes guidelines for group reflection. My hope is that these books will deepen your worship, and enable you to reflect Christ in every facet of your life.

I am deeply indebted to the churches where I have facilitated worship and led training workshops, and to the individuals with whom I have shared these experiences. I am thankful for the many writers and theologians whose work has shaped my thinking. I am very grateful to Margaret Rundle who so carefully and generously edited the manuscript. Finally, without the support of my family, especially my wife and partner in ministry, Debbie, my writing ministry would not exist. Any value that may be found in this series is simply an overflow of the immense value that I have received from others.

May God be your teacher as you embark on this journey of *Learning to Live*.

---

[2] John 10:10

INTRODUCING the JOURNEY

LEARNING
to BELONG

If anyone says, I love God, and hates a brother or sister, he is a liar, because the person who doesn't love a brother or sister who can be seen can't love God, who can't be seen.
– 1 John 4:20 CEB

We are psychologically, emotionally, cognitively, and spiritually hardwired for connection, love, and belonging. Connection, along with love and belonging (two expressions of connection), is why we are here, and it is what gives purpose and meaning to our lives. – Brené Brown

At six in the morning on January 28, 2012, after 25 days in the cruel Antarctic, the South African team of Braam Malherbe and Peter van Kets completed the Scott-Amundsen Centenary Race to the South Pole. They crossed the line in third place, along with the British pair. Only four out of the original seven teams reached the finish.

Without the help of "Team Mission Impossible" as the South Africans were known, the British team would never have made it. Just before reaching the halfway mark, one of their members fractured his arm, making it impossible for him to pull his sled with its seventy kilogram load. But, with each South African willing to carry an extra nine kilograms, the British were able to continue. It was a kind and sacrificial act that bonded these four competitors together in the last week of their gruelling journey.[1]

You don't have to trek through the Antarctic to know that this world can feel like a very hostile place. Evil exists and suffering is universal. This reality has led some people to question the existence of God, and others to seek safety in isolation from others. But, as people of faith have discovered through the centuries, it is only as we connect with God, with others, and with our world that we can really be safe. Real security and abundant life flow from knowing that we have a place where we truly and authentically belong. The problem is that a sense of belonging does not come naturally to us. It must be learned.

There are many rituals that can teach us to be at home in God's world, but few are as effective as the gathering of a community for worship. In the first few moments of most Christian worship services, four interrelated practices teach us how to learn to belong – the choice to *gather*, the *call to worship*, *invoking* God's presence, and *greeting* one another. This book explores how these simple acts can show us how to find our place and help one another to be at home in the world.

Like the two teams that finished the race to the South Pole together, we need one another. Sharing life is risky, and it will certainly hurt at times. But, if we're willing to take the chance, we can find life in communities of love, grace and diversity. I pray that you will join me in this journey as we learn how to be at home in God's world together.

---

[1] More information about the South African team's participation in the "toughest race on the planet" can be found at: http://www.myschool.co.za/blog/650-latest-news-on-the-2012-scott-amundsen-centenary-race-to-the-south-pole-braam-malherbe-progress-update (accessed 30 October 2012)

week one

gathering

And let us not neglect our meeting together, as some people do, but encourage one another, especially now that the day of His return is drawing near.
— Hebrews 10:24-25

But the very next thing we should consider is something that easily slips from notice: the very fact that we are here – that on a Sunday morning, one of the few times that the city's streets are quiet and even the steady hum of consumption and production gets a bit quieter, here we find people streaming into a space to gather for worship of the triune God.
— James. K. A. Smith

thought for the week

As the title of Dan Kimball's book suggests, many people have decided that *They Like Jesus, But Not The Church.* But if we engage with Jesus seriously, it doesn't take long to recognize that he drives us back into relationship with other people. We cannot follow Christ alone. Any authentic spiritual quest requires us to journey with others who will support us, challenge us, and help us to change and grow.

Other people are necessary for our health. They function as both mirrors and windows. As mirrors, they reflect back to us our goodness and our brokenness, revealing both our capacity to make a contribution to the world, and the areas of our lives where we need to do more work. As windows, other people open us to new insights and experiences of God and of the world. So, even though you may be wary of the church, you may well want to consider making some kind of faith community an integral part of your own spiritual journey.

In the first moment of any meeting of any group of people a significant thing happens: we gather. Simply by choosing to gather we recognize that we need other people, and we open ourselves to be connected to them and shaped by them. The moment of gathering, mindfully experienced, can lead us into a sense of belonging that can challenge, change and bless us more than we could ever have imagined.

day one

WE ARE WIRED to connect

---

*Then the LORD God said, "It is not good for the man to be alone.
I will make a helper who is just right for him." – Genesis 2:18*

*Without connection there is something dangerous and wrong
about the world. – David Nichols*

to read

Genesis 2:4-8, 18-25

to think about

It was only when I felt alone that I became really afraid. Clinging to the rock face just below the cable station on Table Mountain, I resisted the temptation to look down at the long, sheer drop below me. *People die on this mountain*, I thought. As I searched for my next handhold and tried to balance my weight to climb safely to the next ledge, I kept reminding myself that this was not actually a true rock-climbing expedition. It was more like a tough hike with a few sections of rock-scrambling. Above me I could hear the happy chatter of my wife, my teenage son and our three friends. A voice in my head challenged me: "If you fall, would they even know?" That's when I realized that, as silly as it sounded even to me, I was frightened by what we were doing. It was also the moment when I knew I had to stay more connected with the group.

As soon as I was secure on a flat, stable surface, I called out to the others and asked if I could move into the centre of the group as we continued on. I gladly agreed when one friend offered to carry the backpack with our refreshments. There was no way anyone could have caught me should I have fallen, but just knowing that I would not be isolated gave me confidence. Alone I was afraid. Connected, I was at peace and somehow more secure.

Human beings are sociable creatures. We find our joy and our security in connecting with others. As infants we cannot survive alone, and as adults, we need friends and family to keep us safe and healthy.

In Genesis, just after the world is created, God forms the first human being. As soon as the breath of life enters his clay-formed body, a search begins for a suitable companion for this lone man. All the animals are paraded before him, and he names each one, but none of them is able to be a true friend to him. Finally, God decides to create the perfect match for Adam – another human being who is completely like him, but very different. When the man first sets eyes on the woman, he exclaims in joy, "At last! This one is bone from my bone, and flesh from my flesh!"[1]

This story, written to the Jews who had been conquered and carried into exile by the Babylonians, was meant to reassure God's people that they had not been abandoned. *God had created them to be connected to God and to one another.* As God had not ignored the loneliness of the first human being, so God would not ignore the loneliness of his exiled people.

Science agrees with the Scriptures that we are wired to connect. The University of Miami's Touch Research Institute has conducted extensive studies on the effects of touch on human beings. The results indicate that "...touch lessened pain, improved pulmonary function, increased growth in infants, lowered blood glucose and improved immune

---

[1] Genesis 2:23

function".[2] Connection contributes to our health. Disconnection damages it.

But, we don't need science or the Bible to tell us that we're wired to connect. We know it in the depth of our souls. We also know that we live in a connected universe. Every ecosystem on our planet is a carefully balanced set of relationships between organisms and environment. On every level, from microscopic particles to planets and stars, the universe connects and works together to sustain life.

That's why we cannot find joy, meaning and fulfillment without deep relationships. That's why isolation is used in prisons and prisoner of war camps as the harshest of punishments. That's why, when characters are separated and threatened in horror movies, we find it so terrifying.

No matter how much we may want to be free to satisfy our personal dreams and desires, we all share the longing to know and be known, to love and be loved. That's why Jesus taught that the greatest commandment is to love God and to love our neighbors as we love ourselves. That's why, when Jesus proclaimed that God's Reign had come, he formed a community to show what it looks like.

If we want to find our place in the world, if we long to live a life of meaning, abundance, purpose, fulfillment and joy, we have to learn to belong. It is only as we acknowledge our need to connect, and as we work to create strong relationships with friends, family and neighbors, that we are able to become the people God made us to be – the people we know in our hearts we want to be. When we fail to find a place to truly and honestly belong, we are stunted in our growth toward wholeness, becoming broken and even destructive. Larry Crabb suggests "...that the root of all our personal and emotional difficulties is a lack of togetherness, a failure to

---

[2] Bauer, Mary, *The Importance of Human Touch*, (Published at LivesStrong.com, March 30, 2011): http://www.livestrong.com/article/186495-importance-of-human-touch/?utm_source=popslideshow&utm _medium=a1 (accessed 16 August 2012)

connect that keeps us from receiving life and prevents the life in us from spilling over onto others."[3]

We are wired to connect, but until we learn to make the daily choice to live as connected people, we will never really know the life-giving power of true belonging. And we will miss out on the abundant gifts that can only be found in relationship with others.

to δo

Take some time today to sit still in a quiet place. Begin by closing your eyes and focussing on your breath. Feel the rise and fall of your chest as you inhale and exhale. Then allow your mind to reach out. Become aware of the environment in which you are sitting. Listen for the sounds, feel the temperature, and notice how much life is going on around you. Now allow your mind to reach out even further. Let your thoughts take in your whole country, the world, and even the universe. Sit with this awareness for a few moments and then allow yourself to feel the connectedness of it all. Become aware of God's Spirit moving within you, and within the whole cosmos. Then, when you're ready, open your eyes and prepare to carry this sense of connectedness with you into the rest of your day.

to pray

God of Love, you have made me to connect with you and with others, and I open my heart to love.

---

[3] Crabb, Larry, *Connecting*, (Nashville, Word Publishing, 1997), 32.

day two

connection is frightening

---

*When the woman realized that she could not stay hidden, she
began to tremble and fell to her knees in front of Him. The
whole crowd heard her explain why she had touched Him and
that she had been immediately healed. "Daughter," He said to
her, "your faith has made you well. Go in peace."*
– Luke 8:47-48

*Thus all life itself represents a risk, and the more lovingly we
live our lives the more risks we take. – M. Scott Peck*

to read

Luke 8:43-48

to think about

The person I was most afraid of seeing was my uncle. A few
months before, I had packed up my family and moved to a
small town in South Africa's Eastern Cape. I had thought that
accepting the invitation to join the missionary couple who
lived there was the fulfillment of a dream. We were to
establish a ministry of teaching and evangelism through
music, and I was willing to risk everything on the promise it
offered. Six months later, I returned to my home in
Johannesburg. The dream had evaporated, and I had lost
almost everything in the process. I was ashamed and broken.

Every reunion with friends and family was embarrassing, but I dreaded seeing my uncle above all. He was an intelligent man who did not share my faith, and I assumed that my failure would simply give him a good reason to disparage me and what I believed. I couldn't have been more wrong.

Inevitably the day came when I was visiting my parents and my uncle arrived. As he walked into the room I braced myself for the difficult conversation ahead. But, he shook my hand, smiled and made one simple remark that brought more healing than I could have imagined: "You can't put a price tag on experience." As frightening as it was to reconnect with my friends and family, the connection was the very thing that brought the healing I needed. It was a moment in which I was deeply grateful that I had a family in which I truly belonged.

In Luke's Gospel Jesus is approached by a synagogue leader named Jairus. His daughter is deathly ill, and he begs Jesus to go to his home and heal her. On the way, a woman who has suffered from twelve years of vaginal bleeding sneaks up behind Jesus and touches his robe. She knows that, according to the law, she is unclean. She also knows that anything she touches becomes unclean. But, if she can keep her touch a secret, no one would have to know that she had just defiled this popular rabbi.

But then, Jesus stops and asks who touched him. The woman must have feared the worst as she fell, trembling, at his feet. Now everyone would know what she had done. She had trusted in another person, in the most careful and self-protective way, and now he was putting her on display for all to see. Yet, the shame and judgement that she expected didn't come. By making her touch public, Jesus ensured that everyone now knew that she was no longer unclean. Then, he sent her on her way with his final words of grace: "Your faith has made you well. Go in peace."[1] As terrifying as this small act of connection was, it opened the door to the healing and acceptance that this poor woman needed so desperately. It

---

[1] Luke 8:48

was not just her body that was healed, but her place in the community. Once again, she had a place to belong.

Today, the spread of social media has made our private lives public as never before. We are connected to more people than ever, and we often know more about them and their movements than we could have in the past. Yet, we seem unable to shake the sense of aloneness in the midst of the crowd. As M. Scott Peck writes:

> Trapped in our tradition of rugged individualism, we are an extraordinarily lonely people. So lonely, in fact, that many cannot even acknowledge their loneliness to themselves, much less to others. Look at the sad, frozen faces all around you and search in vain for the souls hidden behind masks of makeup, masks of pretense, masks of composure.[2]

Perhaps, in part, this loneliness has arisen from a growing fear of connection. We are in danger of losing the ability to be vulnerable – which is essential to human relationships – because we are so afraid of betrayal, rejection, lies and abuse. We would prefer not to have to take responsibility for others, and we are afraid that we will be asked to give more than we can. We are also very familiar with our own flaws, and we know that we will inevitably fail those who risk connecting with us. We have convinced ourselves that if we don't belong, we can avoid the pain of hurting and being hurt. As Simon and Garfunkel sang, "If I'd never loved, I never would have cried."[3]

We may free ourselves from tears by rejecting community, but we also protect ourselves from joy, healing and the possibility of becoming our truest, most whole selves. This is not to say that it is wrong to be careful around other people. It is healthy to take precautions to save ourselves from unnecessary pain. But, when our self-care turns into selfish disregard for others, we become hard and broken. When our

---

[2] Peck, M. Scott, *The Different Drum*, (London, Rider, 1987), 58.

[3] Simon, Paul, *I Am A Rock*, from the album *Sounds of Silence*, by Simon & Garfunkel (Columbia Records, 1966).

quest for independence becomes an arrogant determination to need no one else, our relationships become dysfunctional and lifeless.

Love is both our most basic human need, and our most glorious human capacity. But, we cannot love alone. As frightening as it can be to open ourselves to love, it is far more frightening to lose the capacity for love. As painful as belonging can be, having nowhere to belong is far worse.

to do

As you think about what it means for you to be part of a community of faith, give yourself enough time today to start a process of honest confession and deep healing. Sit quietly and think about times when others have hurt you. Acknowledge the pain, sit with it for a moment, and then release it to God. Then, remember times when you have failed others. Acknowledge any sense of guilt or shame you feel, sit with these feelings for a moment, and then release them to God as well. Now ask God to heal you, and to release his love in your heart again. Confess any ways that you have separated yourself from others, or resisted finding your place in a community of faith. Open yourself to God's grace and acceptance, and begin to feel what it might be like to choose to belong again. Finish with a prayer of thanksgiving for God's love that comes to you through other people.

to pray

When I separate myself from others, O God, forgive me, and teach me to love and be loved again.

δay thREE

OVERCOMING OUR fEAR (1)

As Jesus was walking along, He saw a man named Matthew sitting at his tax collector's booth. "Follow Me and be My disciple," Jesus said to him. So Matthew got up and followed Him. Later, Matthew invited Jesus and His disciples to his home as dinner guests, along with many tax collectors and other disreputable sinners.
– Matthew 9:9-10

[T]he church...exists to save [people] from the great danger of wasting their lives, becoming something less than and other than they were intended to be, gaining the world but losing their souls. – Brian D. McLaren

to REaδ
Matthew 9:9-12; 10:1-4

to thɪnk aBout
I will never forget standing in line to vote in South Africa's first democratic election. The queues on April 27, 1994 were long and often moved slowly, but the atmosphere was hopeful and friendly. It was easy to chat to strangers, and many residents brought refreshments to those who were waiting on the streets outside their homes. Our society was no longer imprisoned by walls of racial and cultural division, and we

believed that we could become what Archbishop Emeritus Desmond Tutu called "The Rainbow Nation".

In the decades since, we have had to face the deep scars that still remain, and racism has often raised its head. We are not yet whole, but that day of standing together under the African sun was a deeply healing moment. It continues to offer a vision of what is possible, and it still reminds us that, for better or worse, we all belong together. Some of our best moments have been when we have remembered that day, and some of our worst have been when we have forgotten or questioned it. The truth that is hinted at here is this: we do not become a community once we have found healing; *we are healed when we choose to be in community.*

Matthew – the tax collector who became an apostle of Jesus – knew this truth first hand. The decision to accept work as a tax collector in first century Israel was a choice to reject the community into which you had been born. Tax collectors were seen as traitors. By choosing to work for Rome or, in Matthew's case, for the hated King Herod, tax collectors had made themselves unclean – condemned by their peers and rejected by God. We can only assume that Matthew had lost faith in the community of God's people enough that he no longer cared whether he belonged or not.

Then, one day, everything changed. As Jesus walked past the tax collection booth, he addressed Matthew in a way that would have been completely unfamiliar. There were no curses and no angry accusations. Unlike others who would have vented their hatred at this apostate, Jesus offered a simple invitation: "Follow me and be my disciple."[1] We cannot know what went through Matthew's head in the moment in which he decided to accept, but he must have known that he was stepping back into a life of community. Jesus had other disciples with him when he made the offer, and immediately after his response, Matthew held a dinner party in which he introduced Jesus to his (rather shady) friends. Later, when Jesus sent out his twelve apostles to preach and heal,

---

[1] Matthew 9:9

Matthew was among them. His disillusionment with community had been replaced by faith and commitment. Perhaps all Matthew needed was a vision of community that was worthy of the name – and once he had found it, the choice to belong healed him.

Jesus did not come to start a church, but his mission cannot be accomplished by individuals alone. The centre of Jesus' preaching was the Reign of God – a community of peace, justice and love built on the Jubilee vision of Leviticus 25.

This section of the Old Testament law lays the basic foundations for creating true community. Each person was called to care for the well-being of others, and no one was able to exploit or oppress another. Every fifty years land was to be returned to its original owners, slaves were to be freed and debts were to be remitted. The law of the Jubilee was a way to ensure that the community would regularly be brought back to the basic values of equality, justice, mutual support and shared life. When Jesus declared his mission in his hometown synagogue, he borrowed the words of Isaiah's prophecy and stated that he had come to proclaim "the year of the Lord's favor".[2] Most scholars agree that this is a reference to the Jubilee.

God's Jubilee dream of a loving, compassionate, healing community is the foundation of the church's existence. The church does not exist for its own sake, but is meant to be a community formed around Jesus' vision of God's Reign. It is not, in itself, the Reign of God, but, at its best, it strives to reflect God's dream, and embody God's love and grace as Jesus did. Unfortunately the church has often failed to live up to its calling, and has driven many people away from the deep, healing connections it can offer. Nevertheless, when we acknowledge our longing for a community that demonstrates the possibility of knowing and sharing God's gracious love, the Church remains one of the few options that can possibly meet our need. As Philip Yancey writes, "I rejected the church for a

---

[2] See Luke 4:16-21

time because I found so little grace there. I returned because I found grace nowhere else."[3]   Or, as Brian McLaren so powerfully stated, "[V]ery literally, churches save lives."[4]

The first step, then, in overcoming our fear of connection, is to open our hearts and minds to God's Jubilee dream, and imagine what it would be like to belong to a community that seeks to live it out.

to do

Read through the instructions for the Jubilee celebration in Leviticus 25:8-17, 35-43. Take a moment to imagine what it would be like to live in a community that cares for one another like this. Imagine what the world would be like if God's Jubilee dream was the way we lived. Then, think about the church as you have experienced it. Allow your feelings to arise, and compare them with your feelings about the Jubilee dream. Now separate the church and God's Reign in your mind. Recognize that they are very different things. Finally, think about becoming part of a church that tries (and often fails) to cling to the dream of God's Reign. How do you feel about learning to belong in such a community? Carry this sense of belonging with you through the day, and allow it to direct all your relationships and decisions.

to pray

Fill my heart with your dream of Jubilee, O God, and let it heal any fear I have of connecting with others.

---

[3] Yancey, Philip, *What's So Amazing About Grace?* (Grand Rapids, Zondervan, 1997), 16.

[4] McLaren, Brian D. *A New Kind of Christianity,* (New York, Harper One, 2010), 162.

OVERCOMING OUR fear (2)

After breakfast Jesus asked Simon Peter, "Simon son of John, do you love Me more than these? " "Yes, Lord," Peter replied, "You know I love You." "Then feed My lambs," Jesus told him.
– John 21:15

Love can soothe what love has burned. – Amy Grant

to read
John 21:14-22

to think about

"I've been arrested...for shoplifting!"

I couldn't believe what I was hearing. The woman on the other end of the telephone line was a committed member of my church, and one of the most gracious and honest people I knew. As she told me her story, I learned that she had been looking for underwear in a large department store. Finding nothing she liked, she moved on, but, unknown to her, the clasp of a bra had caught on the strap of her handbag where it stayed as she moved through the store. When she decided to leave, she was arrested at the exit by a zealous security guard.

"My first reaction was embarrassment, and I laughed it off. But, he was serious and wouldn't listen to my explanation," she cried.

I did my best to reassure her, and drove straight to the store where I managed to convince the manager that they had made a terrible mistake. When I arrived at the police station to secure her release from jail, I found her in a cell chatting comfortably with a number of other women. As she left, they all waved goodbye and asked her to keep praying for them. She explained to me the crimes that these women had committed, and described how she had shared her faith and counseled them. In this most unwelcoming situation she had made herself at home, and had become a servant and confidant to these broken women.

As I listened to her story, I was reminded of the miraculous connections that can happen when one person is willing to reach out to others in love. If ever I had seen the grace and acceptance of Christ at work in another human being, it was as I stood at the bars of that prison cell.

On the night of his arrest, one of Jesus' closest friends pretended that they were strangers. In trying to stay close to Jesus, Peter had found himself in the courtyard of the high priest's house, where he was recognized as a disciple. But, when he was questioned, he vehemently denied knowing Jesus.

A few days later, Peter and some friends encountered the resurrected Jesus on the beach. Although he had every reason to hold a grudge against Peter, Jesus took the initiative to restore their relationship and to free Peter from any guilt.

Jesus could have decided that the community he had established had become threatening. He could have nursed his pain and built a wall around his heart, and he could have used his last few weeks on earth to continue his mission alone. But, of course, he didn't do that. He insisted on reclaiming his place of belonging among his friends, and he continued to welcome them into deep connection with himself.

All relationships are painful. The more we love another person, the more vulnerable we become, and the more likely it is that they will hurt us. In our fear of being wounded, we often approach others cautiously, waiting for some guarantee that they will be safe for us before we commit to relationship. But, rather than guarantee our safety, this strategy simply guarantees that we will never find the community we long for. In order to find a safe place, we need to *become a safe place for others first.*

If we want to find a community in which we can be loved and accepted just as we are, we must reach out to others in love and acceptance. If we want companions who will stay connected with us, even when we are at our worst, we need to learn to choose connection even when we don't feel like it, or when those around us are hard to love. As the famous prayer of St. Francis of Assisi, asks:

> O Divine Master, grant that I may not so much seek to be consoled, as to console; to be understood, as to understand; to be loved, as to love.[1]

If we allow our fear to keep us from love, love will never find us. But, if we allow love to drive out our fear,[2] we will be hurt – that much is inevitable – but love will "soothe what love has burned."[3]

This is not to deny that some people and groups become abusive. Dysfunctional communities do exist, and their claims on members can become dangerous, destructive and imprisoning. It is unwise, however, to use these extremes as an excuse to reject community altogether. There are plenty of communities that strive for health, mutual support and acceptance, and it is well worth the effort to seek out such a group and take the initiative to find belonging.

The challenge of community is to risk stepping out of our

---

[1] For the full text of this well-known prayer see this Wikipedia entry: http://en.wikipedia.org/wiki/Prayer_of_Saint_Francis.

[2] See 1 John 4:18

[3] Grant, Amy, *You're Not Alone*. Written by Dennis Morgan, Simon Climie and Rob Fisher, © 1991 Little Shop of MorganSongs (BMI), adm. By Morgan Music Group, Inc./Chrysalis Music Ltd./Rondor Music Ltd., adm. by Almo Music Corp. (ASCAP). From the Album *Heart In Motion*.

self-protection, accept the necessary pain of being together, and embrace the growth, the healing and the gifts that such connection offers. As Rev. Dr Peter Storey has observed, "the togetherness of real community is a costly thing to achieve, but the isolation which is the alternative is much more destructive of our souls".[4] It is worth embracing the "little death" of togetherness in order to achieve the "little resurrection" of belonging.

to ∂o

Take a moment, before going out into your day, to imagine what it would be like to belong to a caring, loving and healing community. Imagine taking the initiative to reach out to others with acceptance, becoming a safe place for them first. Then, imagine staying committed to them even when misunderstandings or differences create hurt. Allow yourself to feel the pain, but also the liberation of knowing you are part of a group that accepts you at your worst as well. Hold these feelings in your heart as you seek to let your guard down a little more with a few other people. Now go out into the day and try to be more intentionally welcoming to everyone you meet.

to pRay

As you have taken the initiative in loving me, O God, teach me to reach out to others first.

---

[4] This sentiment is one that Rev. Dr Storey has expressed many times in his decades of ministry, most often with respect to justice and racial reconciliation in both pre- and post-apartheid South Africa. This wording comes from private email correspondence with the author in May 2012.

day five

worship teaches us to connect

Peter told them, "You know it is against our laws for a Jewish man to enter a Gentile home like this or to associate with you. But God has shown me that I should no longer think of anyone as impure or unclean. So I came without objection as soon as I was sent for." – Acts 10:28,29

In the liturgy, then, we are invited into a deep union with one another, which is achieved through a deep union with the God who is the ultimate source of our unity. – Susan J. White

to read
Acts 10:9-35, 44-45

to think about
How does a drug-addicted, alcoholic, mother-to-be find her way back to life? In her funny and moving book, *Traveling Mercies – Some Thoughts On Faith*, Anne Lamott describes how she found the answer to this question for herself. At age thirty, she was a struggling writer, addicted to alcohol and pills, living on a houseboat in Sausalito, San Francisco. Most Sundays she would find her way to the flea market in Marin City, a dusty, impoverished community across the freeway from her home. On some days, she would be drawn by the music to a small church across the street from the flea

market. It was a small, poor community, but the people were warm and welcoming. At first, she would just stand in the doorway, and flee as soon as the sermon began, but after a while, she began to step inside, sitting alone on one of the folding chairs. But always the music seemed to envelope and comfort her.

When she decided to abort her pregnancy, she experienced an intense sadness and some heavy bleeding. But, she discovered an almost tangible sense of Christ's presence – a feeling that followed her around for days. A week later, she returned to the little church, and stayed right through the sermon. Once again she felt the comfort of being carried by the heartfelt worship of the people. When she got home that day, tearful and broken, she finally allowed Jesus into her life. From then on she hardly ever missed a Sunday.[1]

The church is a community, not because we are all alike, not because we have a lot in common, not because we are all saintly and perfectly gracious. The church is a community because we know that we are all broken and flawed, and we need a place to learn to love, to forgive, to accept, to change and to live well. As Anne Lamott describes it:

> [T]hat is why I have stayed so close to [my church] – because no matter how bad I am feeling, how lost or lonely or frightened, when I see the faces of the people at my church, and hear their tawny voices, I can always find my way home.[2]

In the book of Acts, the apostle Peter discovers how wide God's grace really is. In a dream he is challenged to eat all sorts of foods, both permitted and forbidden. When he protests, he is instructed not to call unclean what God calls clean. Immediately after this vision, Peter is invited to the home of a Roman army officer named Cornelius. Although Jewish law forbids him from entering the house of a Gentile,

---

[1] For the details of her story, see: Lamott, Anne, *Traveling Mercies – Some Thoughts on Faith,* (New York, Pantheon Books, Kindle Edition, 1999), 43-55.

[2] Ibid, 55.

the dream leads Peter to believe that God has sent him, and so he preaches to the people who have gathered in Cornelius' home. While he is still speaking, God's Spirit falls on them, and Peter realizes that God has brought the Gentiles into the new Christ-following community. In every part of this story, it is the act of prayer and worship that makes the creation of this new, diverse church possible.[3]

The impact of a worshipping community on the lives of its members, and of the surrounding neighborhood, should never be underestimated. One of the most significant characteristics of worship is the way it teaches us to create safe places of belonging for one another. Simply the fact that we have gathered – at a time we didn't choose, with people with whom we may not ordinarily associate – offers us a vision of a different way of living.

As we meet in a place filled with stories, images, vocabulary, symbols and rituals that speak of God's Reign, we begin to imagine living together in a world of justice, peace and love. As we sing, pray, listen to the Scriptures, share in the sacramental meal, and possibly enjoy a cup of coffee afterward, we get to know one another, to make allowances for each other, and to work at finding common ground. Our worship offers us a vision of God's Reign which includes all people, and then teaches us to become what we have envisioned – however imperfectly.

Each week as we meet together for worship we are there because we have made the choice to go against the rampant individualism of our society. We are there because we have chosen to align ourselves with something bigger than ourselves. We are there because we want to make a contribution for the sake of others. And we are there because we want our lives to have meaning, we want to matter to God and live with a fulfilling sense of purpose.

This means that we do not come just to "get something out". We gather because we know that our presence makes a difference. When we fail to meet, our absence makes the

---

[3] The whole story is dramatically recounted in Acts 10 and 11.

singing a little softer, the gathering a little smaller, and the commitment of the community to one another a little weaker. But, when we make the effort to meet, our presence uplifts others, affirms our life together, and provides additional energy to make the worship more meaningful, more passionate and more transforming.

Simply by choosing to be there, we learn that our lives matter to one another. By gathering with those who are different from us, we proclaim that all people are loved and included in God's family. As we meet, week after week, we learn to become a safe place for one another, and we discover the joy that comes from working together to make God's Reign a little more visible in our world through our small community of worship.

to ðo

Reflect on your experience of worship. Do you find it difficult to gather with others, or is it a joy? Think about those who are different from you, those whom you wish were not in your church, or with whom you would prefer not to gather. How can you learn to accept and love them? Now think about the difference it makes – to you and others – when you choose to be at church each week, and the effect it has when you stay away. Can you make a commitment today to be at church as often as you can manage, and allow it to teach you to belong in a worshipping community?

to pRay

Thank you, O God, for the gift of worship that teaches me about your inclusive love, and how to share that love with others.

day six

the gifts of belonging

"Now swear to me by the LORD that you will be kind to me and my family since I have helped you. Give me some guarantee that when Jericho is conquered, you will let me live, along with my father and mother, my brothers and sisters, and all their families." "We offer our own lives as a guarantee for your safety," the men agreed. "If you don't betray us, we will keep our promise and be kind to you when the LORD gives us the land." – Joshua 2:12-14

[C]hurch has filled in me a need that could not be met in any other way. – Philip Yancey

to read

Joshua 2:1-24

to think about

It was painful to say goodbye, but beneath the grief at our parting was a quiet gratitude for the journey that had brought us to this place. After her first uncertain visits to our church, Betty[1] had slowly become an integral part of our little community. When I had met her I had known I was looking at a woman who had been battered by life. In the weeks that

---

[1] Not her real name.

followed I discovered that she had a capacity for deep and sacrificial love, as evidenced by her attentive care of her two children. But, I also learned that she had never received in return the love she so willingly gave. Her loveless and violent marriage had become a prison from which she could find no escape.

But that had been a couple of years ago. Now, she was strong, happy, free, and leaving for a home in a new country where she had family. She had a job waiting, and the assurance of good education and health care for her children. She had survived the traumatic end of her marriage, and had found the courage to face life on her own. As we prayed for her in her last Sunday service with us, she looked around the church with tears in her eyes, and thanked this small group of believers for loving her back to wholeness. Her story is just one of many that have convinced me that community holds immense gifts for those who are willing to receive them.

Trevor Hudson writes: "Clearly, the climate for growth and deepening in discipleship is community. We cannot become the persons God wants us to be without experiencing divine and human relationships."[2] Again and again I have watched as people who have been broken and discarded by life have found a place of safety, healing and belonging among God-seekers. This should not surprise us – it is simply the manifestation in our own lives of an event that occurs regularly in the Scriptures.

In the second chapter of the book of Joshua we are introduced to a prostitute by the name of Rahab. When the Israelite leader sent two spies across the Jordan River to gather information about the fortified town of Jericho, Rahab sheltered and protected them. In return, the spies promised to save her and her family when the city was conquered.

We cannot know why Rahab decided to help the invaders against her own people. Even if it was nothing more than a self-protective strategy, it would seem to reveal that she felt

---

[2] Hudson, Trevor, *Signposts to Spirituality*, (Cape Town, Struik Christian Books, 1995), 71.

no loyalty to her countryfolk, and therefore no real sense of belonging. But everything changed when she was welcomed into the Israelite community. As a foreigner and a prostitute, she should have been   kept apart, but instead she was accepted and integrated. As her story unfolds we discover that she married a prominent Israelite man, and became one of the ancestors of both King David and Jesus.[3]   Rahab's story demonstrates how significantly a community can impact an individual life in positive ways.

If we believe that all people are created in God's image,[4] we must acknowledge that we learn to know God more deeply in community than we can alone. Each person reflects an aspect of God's image that is unique and that adds to our understanding of God. This is why Jesus taught that his presence is best known when we gather.[5]

But we also become our best selves when we find a place to truly belong. In order to heal from life's wounds, we need a safe group of companions who can cry with us, pray for us, hold our questions, and nurture us back to health. In order to experiment, fail and learn we need the safety which allows us to stretch ourselves and discover what we are capable of. Larry Crabb boldly expresses it this way: "...the surest route to overcoming problems and becoming the people we were meant to be is reconnecting with God and with our community."[6]

In addition, belonging frees us from self-centered, immature individualism. Without the maturity to put ourselves aside for the sake of others, we may meet but we never really *gather*, we may create congregations, but we never experience true *community*. It may feel good for a while to care for no one but ourselves, it may mean that we can more easily accumulate wealth and possessions, it may guarantee that we never have to delay gratification, but it will

---

[3] See Matthew 1:5

[4] Genesis 1:27

[5] Matthew 18:20

[6] Crabb, Larry, *Connecting*, (Nashville, Word Publishing, 1997), 32.

never enable us to become the most whole and mature version of ourselves.

Maturity brings the wisdom and humility to know that we need others as much as they need us. It teaches us what we have to offer and what we lack. It enables us to take ourselves less seriously, to enjoy goodness more freely, and to appreciate others more readily without needing to change them to fit our agendas. Once we have embraced the maturity that belonging brings, we start to care for one another deeply, and we learn to love and be loved, to know and be known, to heal and be healed in ways that lead us into abundant, meaningful life.

to ÐO

Think back over your life, and remember times when you have been healed or blessed by others. Take note of how you felt in those times, and what it was about your connection that made them so special.

Now reflect on what you need in order to grow, learn and become your best self right now. Think about how a community could potentially meet those needs. Also think about what contributions you could make to help others to grow.

Make a commitment to open yourself to learning and receiving from everyone you meet today, and to giving back to them whatever support, grace, insight, laughter or comfort you can.

to pRAY

Thank you God that you have given me companions to reveal yourself to me, to heal me and to help me become my best self.

Living a "gathered" Life

They worshiped together at the Temple each day, met in homes for the Lord's Supper, and shared their meals with great joy and generosity – all the while praising God and enjoying the goodwill of all the people. And each day the Lord added to their fellowship those who were being saved. – Acts 2:46-47

When we live in God in the world, we see everything, whether on the other side of the world or down the street, in a new way. The primary lens is no longer our family background, our personality, prejudices, worries or subculture; it is now the love of God for every person. – Mark Labberton

to read

Acts 2:41-47, 4:32-35

to think about

For this woman, the Rwandan genocide was deeply personal. Forty-one family members, among them her own children, had been killed. As a result of multiple rapes, she now faced a life with HIV/Aids. Yet, when she was able to return to her village, she could not ignore the children who had been orphaned by the violence. As part of her care for those around her, she took in two boys, one of whom was also HIV positive, to raise as her own sons. She knew that some of the people in her village participated in the killing of her family and the rape of her body. But she also knew that she had to choose whether to live the rest of her life in bitterness and hatred or in forgiveness and service of others. She chose to forgive, and now, by God's grace, she and her adopted sons seek daily to love her neighbors.[1]

Those of us who live above the breadline have grown used to being served. We have come to expect that companies will scramble over one another to gain our attention and our money. We demand that products, services and marketing be tailored to our preferences. We even assume that religious groups will compete for our membership by meeting our specific generational, musical and theological needs. But, this pandering to our desires has not helped our souls. We have grown narcissistic and overloaded by choice.[2]

The antidote to this unhealthy self-centeredness is to allow belonging to teach us to become contributors, rather than consumers. When we take our place in a faith community we commit to sharing in its mission to embody God's grace, justice and love. This means that we choose to follow the foot-washing example of Jesus,[3] offering our time, skills, expertise, friendship, attention and resources to friends and neighbors. As we learn to serve and give, our souls soften and awaken, our connection with the world expands and deepens, and our joy multiplies.

The New Testament church, described in the book of Acts, demonstrates the power that a gathered community can have on the lives of its members and of the surrounding society. The activities in which this group of new believers engaged each day were not dramatic. They ate together and prayed together. They shared their resources and possessions with

---

[1] A friend of author Mark Labberton's met this woman in Rwanda. Her story is told in Mark Labberton's book *The Dangerous Act of Worship*, (Downers Grove, Illinois, IVP Books, 2007), 164.

2 For the impact of the "Paradox of Choice" on our lives see the excellent TED talk by psychologist and author Barry Schwartz at this url: http://tinyurl.com/cvfhxky.

[3] See John 13:1-15

one another. They listened to the teaching of the apostles and remembered Jesus in the breaking of bread. They worshipped in the Temple and gave hospitality to those within and outside of their community. But, through this daily choice to live as a gathered people they brought tremendous blessing and healing to others, and their community grew and flourished. When we choose to be part of a gathered community, and mindfully add our small efforts to those of others, we begin to experience the presence and wholeness of God, and we become carriers of God's abundant life to those around us.

In the simple choice to gather, we become people who believe that there is more to life than the individualistic quest for personal fulfillment and freedom – people who are willing to allow the grand vision of God's Reign to be the central focus of our lives. And this belief drives us into deeper relationship with our companions in Christ. When we regularly choose to gather with others at church, we are intentionally reaching beyond ourselves and seeking to make connections with other people. We are intentionally striving to serve and be served, to belong and create a place of belonging for others.

The gathering of Christ-followers in times of worship is neither an escape, nor an end in itself. It is a learning time, in which we are taught to be Christlike people of grace, hospitality and service. Then, having learned these skills through our worship, we carry them out into the rest of our week, embracing each day as an opportunity to live the connections we have discovered at church, to serve, love, forgive, welcome and connect with our neighbors, colleagues, friends – and even those we might think of as our enemies.

If Mother Teresa was right that the worst human disease is that of being unwanted, the choice to gather is the prescription that heals and restores us.[4] But, this belonging

---

[4] The exact wording of this quote is as follows: "The biggest disease today is not leprosy or tuberculosis, but rather the feeling of being unwanted." According to the Wikiquote website Malcolm Muggeridge attributes these words to Mother Teresa in his book *Something Beautiful for God*, published in 1971. See this url: http:// en.wikiquote.org/wiki/Mother_Teresa (accessed 23 August 2012)

does not always come naturally to us. It must be learned. That is why the decision to gather week after week is prophetic, transforming and healing. Our contribution to the gathered community reaches beyond us as individuals, and makes the world a more whole and hospitable place.

to do

Take a moment to reflect on what you have experienced and learned this week. Make a special note of any specific actions that you have committed to, or that you can make a part of your life. Give thanks for God's gift of community, and for the invitation to belong and create a space of belonging for others.

Now create a "gathered-life plan" for yourself. Think about specific ways that you can be more involved in your local church and make a commitment to follow through. Then think about ways that you can take what you learn in worship each week into the rest of your life. Make a list of people that you can reach out to more intentionally, or ministries that you can contribute time, skills or resources to. Keep this plan in your Bible, your diary or on your computer and return to it regularly.

to pray

O God, teach me to offer the belonging I have found in you to my friends and neighbors.

to explore together

ICE BREAKER

Tell the story of a gathering with other people in which you had a lot of fun, felt really welcomed, or learned a lot.

WORSHIP

Take a moment to look around the group and become aware of how special it is that you have gathered together. Then, remember any members who are not present. Spend a moment in prayer, giving thanks for your group and your gathering. Sing or read a gathering hymn or poem together.

Allow a moment for each person to share a specific prayer request either for themselves or someone else, and then pray for these needs together.

Close with the Lord's Prayer and singing or reading a hymn affirming the gift of the faith community.

READING

Psalm 133

DISCUSSION QUESTIONS

1. What stood out for you in this week's reflections?
2. Share stories of harmony, and the lack of it, in the community of faith. How have these experiences affected you?
3. Do you wrestle with the fear of connecting with others? How does this affect you? What can you do to overcome it?
4. What benefits can be found in learning to belong in a community of faith? How does worship help us receive these benefits?
5. How can you commit a little more to living a "gathered" life?

week two

called

---

*But you are a chosen race, a royal priesthood, a holy nation, a
people who are God's own possession. You have become this
people so that you may speak of the wonderful acts of the one
who called you out of darkness into his amazing light.*
– 1 Peter 2:9 CEB

*This is the true joy in life, the being used for a purpose
recognized by yourself as a mighty one; the being thoroughly
worn out before you are thrown on the scrap heap; the being a
force of Nature instead of a feverish selfish little clod of
ailments and grievances complaining that the world will not
devote itself to making you happy.*
– George Bernard Shaw

thought for the week

In his book, *The 8th Habit*, Stephen R. Covey speaks about the "deep, innate, almost inexpressible yearning within each one of us to find our voice in life."[1] As human beings we are designed to look for meaning in the world and in our own lives. We cannot help but wonder what our purpose for being might be. Many of us seek this meaning primarily within ourselves. It is not wrong to do this, but if that's as far as we go, we will inevitably be disappointed. The reason for this is that we cannot be satisfied with just any purpose. Somewhere deep within us, we know that our reason for being must be more than a selfish desire for self-fulfillment. It must connect us with others and must make a difference to the world. Our purpose must be more than just *our* voice. It must flow out of a sense of *call* – a conviction that our lives have been created by God to become part of *God's voice*. We need to know that we are part of something bigger than ourselves that participates in God's purpose for creation.

This is why Christian worship begins with a *call to worship*. At the very start of our gatherings, we are called to know God and be known by God. As we respond to this call, we choose to direct our attention and energy to the practices of our worship so that they can teach us what it means to live as God's Called People. We do this in community because we believe that only as we work together can we truly make a difference. And, as we learn to live out our calling together, we discover that sharing in God's mission gives us a place to truly belong.

---

[1] Covey, Stephen R., *The 8th Habit – From Effectiveness To Greatness,* (New York, Simon & Schuster, 2004), 5.

WE ARE WIRED FOR PURPOSE

Looking at the man, Jesus felt genuine love for him. "There is still one thing you haven't done," He told him. "Go and sell all your possessions and give the money to the poor, and you will have treasure in heaven. Then come, follow Me." – Mark 10:21

[The one who] knows the "why" for his [or her] existence...will be able to bear almost any "how". – Viktor E. Frankl

to read
Mark 10:17-22

to think about

In a concentration camp where prisoners live or die on the whims of feared authority figures, and where the hope of survival is small, what reason could there be for not ending one's own life sooner rather than later? For many of the men with whom Viktor Frankl was imprisoned during World War II, the answer was none, and they chose to commit suicide as a result.

But, at least two deaths were prevented when the other prisoners rallied around those in despair and helped them to find a reason to live. In one case, the man had a beloved child who was waiting for him in a foreign country. The other man was a scientist who had written a series of books that were unfinished. No one else would have been capable of completing this work, and so the possibility of returning to the project pulled him out of his hopelessness. For both of these men, what stopped them from taking their own lives was the realization that they had a purpose to fulfill, a "why" that gave them the strength and courage to face the daily "how" of life in a concentration camp.[1]

If there is one thing human beings fear it is the thought of a random world. We are wired to make meaning of our world and of our own lives, and if we can find no "why" we easily fall into despair and depression. Without meaning, we believe our lives have no value. But when we are able to make sense of the world, to find a reason for our existence, we are able to face the most difficult tragedies, the most costly sacrifices, and the most fearful challenges.

Our quest for meaning is more than just a desire that the world should make sense. We also long to feel that we have a contribution to make. In their inspiring book, *The Art of Possibility*, Rosamund and Benjamin Zander speak of a "disease" they call "second fiddle-itis". Second violinists often feel that their role in an orchestra is unimportant and that they make little contribution to the music. They are often unnoticed by the conductor, even if their instruments are out of tune. As a result, these musicians may stop practicing, and lose passion for their music. On the other hand, first oboe players are unlikely to stop maintaining their instrument or to miss rehearsals. As Benjamin Zander puts it: "In all my years of conducting, I do not believe I have ever known a first oboe to be late for rehearsal. Is it because the oboe has to be there at the beginning to tune everyone to the A?"[2]

As I travel across South Africa I often ask the groups of people I train how many of them would like the world to be worse off when they die than it was when they were born. No

---

[1] The stories of these two prevented suicides are told in Viktor Frankl's book, *Man's Search For Meaning* (Revised and Updated), (New York, Washington Square Press, 1985), 100-101.

[2] Zander, Benjamin and Rosamund, *The Art of Possibility*, (New York, Penguin Books, 2000), 40-41.

one ever raises a hand, and most people look at me with a
rather confused expression. But, when I ask how many people
want the world to be better off when they die than it was when
they were born, every hand in the room is raised. I have never
met a human being who does not want to make some sort of
positive contribution to the world. We all long to live lives of
significance and purpose, lives of meaning and value. We all
want to leave a positive mark on the world, however small,
that indicates that the world was better off because we were in
it for a while.

But, here is where we sometimes get derailed. There are so
many meanings, so many purposes calling for our attention,
but not all lead us to the satisfaction and fulfillment that we
desire. In the Gospels, a wealthy man came to Jesus with a
longing to be part of something meaningful. "What must I do
to inherit eternal life?" he asked. It's important to remember
that in Jesus' preaching eternal life was not so much about
living forever after death, as it was about becoming part of
God's eternal Reign in this life. After some conversation, Jesus
instructed the man to sell all his possessions and give the
money to the poor, and then to come and follow Jesus. On
hearing this the man walked away despondent, because he
could not face giving away his wealth. He was searching for
meaning, but, while on some level he knew he was looking in
the wrong place, he was unable to risk releasing his riches
and embracing the higher purpose of following Jesus.

The purpose around which we choose to build our lives is
one of the most important decisions we will ever make. Even
deciding to live without any sense of purpose at all is a choice
about the meaning that will shape our lives and how we will
live that meaning out. Sometimes we resist seeking a direction
for our lives because we are afraid that to do so will limit our
freedom. We are concerned that to embrace any higher
purpose will impose a set of restrictions and requirements on
us that will rob us of joy and keep us from exploring life's
possibilities. But, as so many Christ-followers have reported
through the centuries, opening ourselves to God's purpose is
really to become who we were created to be. It is to open

ourselves to the very best life that we could hope to live. In one sense, our primary purpose is simply to become most authentically and completely ourselves. But, if we believe that we are created by God, then finding our truest selves means learning the reason why God created us in the first place.

to do

Reflect on how you have worked with purpose in your life. Have you lived, thus far, with a sense of meaning and direction, or have you preferred to "go with the flow"? Is there any part of you that worries that the world is random and meaningless? Confess these feelings to God and invite God's Spirit to begin to reveal God's meaning in the world and in your life. You may also want to confess any purposes that you have followed that have been unworthy of you, or unfulfilling.

Now, as you go through your day, allow any beauty, truth, goodness, suffering, birth and death that you encounter to speak to you and open your heart to the meaningful nature of the world.

to pray

When I feel afraid that the world is random or that my life is meaningless, help me and heal me, O God.

δay nine

WE aRE aLL CaLLEδ

When Paul and Silas left the prison, they returned to the home of Lydia. There they met with the believers and encouraged them once more. Then they left town. – Acts 16:40

All I know is that...we all need to be aware of our personal calling. What is a personal calling? It is God's blessing, it is the path that God chose for you here on earth. – Paulo Coelho

to Reaδ
Acts 16:12-15, 40

to think aBout

"Members of the Body of Christ, who are now in his name to receive this child, will you so maintain the life of worship and service that [this child], and all the children among you, may grow in grace and in the knowledge and love of God and of his Son Jesus Christ our Lord?"[1]

I spoke these words to a small, rural church as I baptized the newborn child of one the congregants. As they had done many times before, the people replied: "With God's help, we will." Sitting in that congregation was my wife, Debbie. For

---

[1] The Methodist Service Book (Peterborough, Methodist Publishing House, 1975), A8-9.

years she had been a supporter and teammate for my ministry. But, on this Sunday she suddenly recognized that she was called to be a minister in her own right. As the words of the vow were spoken, this sense of call rose up within her. She recognized a longing in her heart to create communities of worship and service in which children could learn to know and love their Creator. That day she began her journey into full-time ministry. Since her ordination she has worked to build communities that fulfill this baptismal vow in the life they share together.

The moment in which we recognize that we are called can be both challenging and fulfilling. Acknowledging our "calledness" changes everything for us. For some, like Debbie, it can mean giving up a career and receiving the church's ordination. For others, work and circumstances may remain unchanged, but in our hearts, in the way we work and live, everything is different.

The churches of the New Testament met in homes. This was the norm for a new, often persecuted, community which had no dedicated buildings. Many of the leaders or hosts of these churches had jobs that they continued alongside their work of ministry. One such person was Lydia. All we can ascertain about her from the Scriptures is that she was a single woman who was a successful cloth merchant. When she heard the Gospel, she was baptized along with her whole household. As far as we can tell, she continued her work, but she also recognized that she had a role to play in spreading the Gospel. And so, she opened her home, and became the founder of a church community.

It is tempting to think of a calling as something that only some people receive, and that always implies some "great" work that we are to do for God. But, this is not the view of the Scriptures. Yes, some are called to prominent and influential roles in church or society. But, those who fulfill more hidden or "ordinary" tasks, are also called. The apostle Paul makes this clear when he compares the church – the Body of Christ –

to a human body.[2] Not all "parts" are visible or strong, but every part is necessary and important for the body to function effectively and to be healthy. Not all callings are "great", but every calling matters – and every person is called in some way.

When we open ourselves to a call, we discover a new sense of belonging in the world, and a stronger sense of meaning and fulfillment in our lives. Our daily routines are no longer random and insignificant. We find that we have a place in the world, a unique contribution to make. Our lives "fit" into a bigger picture and everything we do contributes to the living out of our purpose. Stephen R. Covey, refers to this sense of call as our *voice*:

> When you engage in work that taps your talents and fuels your passion – that rises out of a great need in the world that you feel drawn by conscience to meet – therein lies your voice, your calling, your soul's code.[3]

Whenever I meet someone who has found their unique voice I am always touched by their passion, joy and "aliveness". This is not to say that every called person lives a trouble-free existence – far from it. But, whatever life may throw at us, a sense of call gives us the strength and determination to navigate the joys and the struggles and find meaning, peace, love, celebration and connection.

Every call arises from two sources. In order to hear our personal call, we need to recognize that Someone is calling us. Our lives are not just about ourselves. We have been brought into the world to participate in a purpose that is bigger than we are, and we have a specific contribution to make, however small. In this sense, a call comes from outside of us. Our call connects us with the world, and with the God who both created that world and seeks to save it.

But, our call also comes from within. Every person, sooner

---

[2] See 1 Corinthians 12:12-31

[3] Covey, Stephen R., *The 8th Habit*, (London, Simon & Schuster, 2004), 5.

or later, begins to ask the big questions – "Who am I?" "Why am I here?" "What difference do I make?" As these questions grow within us, we recognize the need to give ourselves to something that can make our lives matter. And, when the voice of our calling begins to echo in our souls, our lives take on a new excitement and significance.

to do

Do you already live with a sense of call, or have you felt that it is only some people who are called? Is your call strong, or has it faded with time or through disappointment? Reflect on how it might feel to live each day from your sense of calling or purpose.

Now take some time to listen. In stillness, open your heart to your own deepest self. If there was nothing stopping you, what contribution would you love to make to the world? Now listen for God's call. Think about what needs in your world challenge or inspire you. Think about the specific teachings of the Gospel that speak to you. Does anything stand out for you? Is there any specific task or principle that you feel particularly moved to live out in your own life?

Don't worry about trying to be too specific at this point. All you want to do is see if any sense of purpose or call – or even just a desire to be called – arises in your heart. If so, write it down so that you return to it from time to time. Now carry this sense of call with you into your day, and keep listening for anything that might add to your "calledness".

to pray

Give me the ears and heart to hear and receive your call, O God.

day ten

sharing in god's dream

"There's a young boy here with five barley loaves and two fish. But what good is that with this huge crowd?" – John 6:9

"I have a dream," God says. "Please help me to realize it." – Desmond Tutu

to read

John 6:1-14

to think about

"If you had told me, even just a few months ago, that I would be doing what I'm doing now, I would have laughed in your face."

These words were spoken, through a wide smile, by a man who had been well known for his racist humor. Even in the years after our first democratic election it was still common to hear jokes with a racial theme in South Africa, especially in rural areas. As a minister of the Gospel, I knew that I was going to have resist this trend. So, whenever I heard someone beginning one of these stories, I made a point of either walking out of the room, or gently interrupting the speaker. In the beginning it was very difficult to take this stand because I really wanted the people to like me, and I would cringe when I saw the surprised and sometimes angry expression on people's faces. But, then a subtle shift started happening. This man began to ask me why I reacted the way I did. Over time he began to grasp my conviction that all people are created in the image of God and worthy of respect, justice and love.

A few months after we had begun talking about these issues, he arrived for a meeting in my home. I could see that he was feeling extremely pleased with himself, and so I asked him if he had anything he wanted to share. He informed me that he had discovered that there was no ministry for the youth in the nearby township, and so he had asked the minister of the Methodist church if he could start a youth group for the black young people of his congregation. That week he was due to hold the first meeting, and he was clearly very excited. He joked about the irony of a recovering white racist driving into the township to share the love of Jesus with black youths. This time, it was easy to laugh along with him, and I celebrated the impact that a simple act of resisting unjust attitudes can have.

The narrative of the Bible portrays God as a Divine Being with a purpose – to save, heal and unite the entire cosmos in the eternal community of God's love.[1] From the outset God has always called women and men to participate in this grand vision. From individuals to families to communities to nations, God has invited human beings to be aligned with God's saving mission. To be called, then, is to live as one whose decisions, actions, motivations and connections are all shaped and inspired by God's saving purpose. To live a called life is to orient our lives around something bigger than ourselves, allowing even our smallest and most insignificant actions to have meaning and contribute to a greater purpose.

It's easy to become overwhelmed when we first sense God's call on our lives. The Jubilee vision of God's Reign of love and justice can feel like an impossible dream when compared with the injustice and suffering in our world. As we think about the energy it takes just to keep our families together, make ends

---

[1] See Ephesians 1:9-10

meet each month and keep our bodies healthy, we may feel that we just don't have the energy or resources to participate in God's mission.

One day a large crowd had gathered around Jesus to hear his teaching. As the day wore on Jesus recognized that the people were hungry and needed to be fed. So, he turned to one of his disciples and asked him where he could find bread for the crowd. There must have been a twinkle in Jesus' eye as he teased his friend, but this did not stop Philip from responding anxiously that they had nowhere near enough money to feed the crowd. Then Andrew noticed a young boy with a small lunch pack. It seemed like a ridiculous contribution, but Jesus took it and somehow turned this child's few loaves and fish into a feast for the crowd.

It must have been a tough decision for this little boy to give up his food. Looking at the crowd he would have expected to receive very little of his lunch back. He must have been tempted to slip away and eat his meal alone. But, instead he offered the little he had for Jesus' use, and it became the catalyst for a miracle. This is all God asks of us as God calls us to participate in God's dream.

We cannot all be Mother Teresa or Nelson Mandela, but we can offer our opportunities, resources and abilities to God. We can undertake the tasks that fill our days mindfully, and with the awareness that even the most mundane act can bring healing and grace into the world. This is surely what Paul had in mind when he wrote that "...whether you eat or drink, or whatever you do, do it all for the glory of God."[2]

This doesn't mean that following Jesus is not very difficult sometimes. At the end of John 6, after the feeding of the crowd and Jesus' proclamation that he is the "Bread of Life", people started drifting away. The call of Jesus, and the implications of his teaching were too much for them. As he watched them leave, Jesus turned to his disciples and asked if they wanted to go too. Peter's response was not very eager, but it has always comforted me when God's call has felt too

---

[2] 1 Corinthians 10:31

hard: "Lord, to whom would we go? You have the words that give eternal life."[3]

Sometimes we hang in there just because we know that the alternative is worse. But, even in those times, it's comforting to remember that we are called by God. Our lives *do* have a reason, a "why", a meaning that is bigger than us. While the specifics may change from person to person, we are all invited to share in God's mission. When we embrace this calling to help God realize God's dream, even the tiniest task becomes filled with love. And that's all that's required to heal the world a little more.

to do

Go back and reread the story of the feeding of the crowd. Put yourself in the place of the little boy. What would you have done, and how would your actions have made you feel? Now see yourself offering Jesus your only food for the day. Imagine watching him break the bread, and then share your food with others. Experience your amazement when you received your share and it was enough.

Now, ask yourself how you can live like this little boy. Think of the time, abilities and resources that you have to offer to God. Throughout today, take every opportunity to give yourself to share in God's dream.

to pray

All that I have and all that I am I offer to you so that I can participate in your dream, O God.

---

[3] John 6:68

day eleven

we are called together

For Abraham will certainly become a great and mighty nation, and all the nations of the earth will be blessed through him.
– Genesis 18:18

Never doubt that a small group of thoughtful, committed citizens can change the world. Indeed, it is the only thing that ever has. – Margaret Mead

to read

Genesis 18:1-19

to think about

The church may have been small, but the gifts they offered made a world of difference to the impoverished families in that town. The soup kitchen had a humble beginning – it fed just a few people once a week. But, as others in our worshipping community heard about it, they wanted to help. Each one seemed to have a different contribution to make. One had contacts with one of the large grocery store chains, and was able to get food that had passed its "sell-by" date. Another person had access to old shipping containers and was able to secure one to convert into a shelter so that soup could still be served when the weather was bad. Another person was a gifted gardener who ran a small nursery and was able to plant a vegetable garden on the church grounds that provided ingredients for the soup. Others were able to contribute time to go to the soup kitchen and serve the unemployed people who came each week for a hot meal. The result of all of these people working together was that the soup kitchen expanded. More people were able to be fed on more days, and the ministry grew into a very significant contribution to that struggling community. It would be clear to anyone who cared to look that this work was not the result of one individual being called – even though it may have begun with only one or two volunteers. Rather, it was as people recognized that they were called as a community, that the work was able to become something important and meaningful.

I have seen similar patterns play out in churches across the country. As small groups of people begin to recognize that they can make a difference, and as they begin to act on that realization, their shared calling leaves a profoundly healing mark on the world. As Dee Hock puts it: "Given the right circumstances, from no more than dreams, determination, and the liberty to try, quite ordinary people consistently do extraordinary things."[1]

From the beginning, when God first started bringing God's dream into being in the world, God called people to share in the dream *together*. After hearing and accepting God's call to leave his home and journey to a foreign land, the man Abraham lived with a sense of purpose. One day as he sat at his tent, he received a divine visitation. It is not clear who the three visitors were who accepted Abraham's hospitality that day, but it is certain that they spoke with the authority of God. They affirmed God's call on Abraham's life, but they also made it clear that it was not an individual calling. Abraham was to give birth to a people, and this divinely called community was to be a blessing to the world.

This is consistent with the rest of the Bible's teaching about God's call. The purpose of God is never primarily for

---

[1] Hock, Dee, *Birth of the Chaordic Age*, (San Francisco, Berrett-Keohler Publishers, 1999), 192.

individuals alone. While there were definitely those, in the Scriptures, who were called to specific and unique roles within the life of God's people – kings, prophets, priests, judges and apostles – these "called ones" were just a *function of the entire community's call*. The tasks of the leaders were designed to enable the whole people – together – to fulfill their calling. The difference between leaders and followers was not a difference in "calledness". They were different only in the specific function they fulfilled within the Called Community.

There are a number of benefits that come from embracing this shared sense of call. Again and again studies have shown that "under the right circumstances, groups are remarkably intelligent, and are often smarter than the smartest people in them."[2] Groups often accomplish more, and with greater intelligence, than individuals alone. In addition, when groups work together, the diversity of abilities, perspectives and personalities releases a creativity that would not be possible for individuals without such stimulation. Finally, when we recognize that "our" call is part of a larger, shared purpose, we learn where we "fit in" and we find a place of belonging in our shared calling.

This is why Paul writes, in his letter to the Romans:

> In His grace, God has given us different gifts for doing certain things well. So if God has given you the ability to prophesy, speak out with as much faith as God has given you. If your gift is serving others, serve them well. If you are a teacher, teach well. If your gift is to encourage others, be encouraging. If it is giving, give generously. If God has given you leadership ability, take the responsibility seriously. And if you have a gift for showing kindness to others, do it gladly.[3]

As each of us discovers our unique sense of call, and where it fits into the shared purpose God has given our community, we discover true belonging, and the ability, together, to make

---

[2] Surowiecki, James, *The Wisdom of Crowds – Why the Many Are Smarter Than the Few,* (London, Little Brown, 2004), xiii.

[3] Romans 12:6-8

a profoundly positive difference to our world – just by being who we are called to be.

to do

The power of expressing our individual calling as part of a larger, shared purpose, is available to us at all times. We are not only part of a community when we are physically gathered together in a church building, or a small group in someone's home. These gatherings teach us to find our place in the Called Community, but we live out our call in the daily routines of our lives. This means that whenever we share life with others in our homes, our work spaces, or our leisure activities, we are able to bring a sense of purpose with us. No matter where we are, or who we are with, we still reflect our part of the church's calling. Today, in every moment when you are with others, try to behave as a called person, who is part of a Called Community. Also, try to allow your gathering with others to teach you more about living as one who is called – even if the others are not people of faith.

to pray

Thank you, O God, for making me a person of purpose who is part of a Called Community.

day twelve

equipped for the call

"I knew you before I formed you in your mother's womb. Before you were born I set you apart and appointed you as My prophet to the nations." – Jeremiah 1:5

The place God calls you to is the place where your deep gladness and the world's deep hunger meet.
– Frederick Buechner

to read

Jeremiah 1:1-10

to think about

"I believe God made me for a purpose – for China. But he also made me fast, and when I run I feel his pleasure. To give it up would be to hold him in contempt." These words were spoken by Eric Liddell in the motion picture *Chariots Of Fire*. The story of his refusal to run in the 100 meter heats because they were being held on a Sunday is well known, as is his world-record-breaking victory in the 400 meters. But Olympic Gold was not all that this humble Christ-follower achieved in his athletic career. His speed on the track earned him the nickname "The Flying Scotsman", and he collected a number of wins in 1924 and 1925 in various national and international competitions. Although these words, created by the script writer for the movie, were never actually spoken by Liddell himself, they do give an accurate view of how God used him to serve others in the name of Christ.

Born to missionary parents in China, Liddell decided to return to the country of his birth in the year following his Olympic triumph. He continued to use his athletic ability as he taught and coached young Chinese students at the schools where he worked, and competed in athletic events in China – which led some to consider him one of China's Olympians. When, during war between the Chinese and Japanese, he was held in an internment camp, he served his fellow prisoners, teaching children, leading Bible studies and organizing sports activities. Although his release was secured by Winston Churchill, he turned the opportunity down, asking that a pregnant woman be released in his place. He finally died in the camp of a brain tumor, just months before the end of hostilities in 1945.[1]

What made Eric Liddell so unique was not his speed on the track, but his character. At races he would shake the hands of all of his opponents before taking his place. In the schools where he taught and in the internment camp where he finally died, he tirelessly served those around him. His athletic ability did not define him, but it did give him opportunities to fulfill God's call on his life, and it remained an effective tool in his work to touch others with the love of Christ.

Millennia before Eric Liddell lived, another young man was called by God to serve in difficult circumstances. When God's call first came to him, Jeremiah doubted his value because of his youth. But, God's word confirmed that he had already been equipped for the task ahead. He had been known by God while still in his mother's womb and before his birth God had already appointed him for the work he was to do. Jeremiah's ministry was a long and painful one. He prophesied the

---

[1] For more information about Eric Liddell's remarkable life, see the entry at Wikipedia (http://en.wikipedia.org/wiki/Eric_Liddell) and this short biography on the Eric Liddell site: http://www.ericliddell.org/ericliddell/biography (both accessed 12 September 2012)

coming conquest of God's people by the Babylonians, and he was persecuted and rejected for speaking the truth. Yet, the book that bears his name contains some of the most hopeful and comforting passages in the Bible.

Reading these stories may not be comforting. Many of us feel inadequate when we hear accounts like these of people whose lives have made such an impact on the world. We wonder how we can possibly measure up if this is what God is asking. It is helpful to remember that many of God's "called ones" felt a similar sense of inadequacy. In Exodus, Moses claimed that he was not eloquent enough.[2] As we have seen, Jeremiah felt that he was too young.[3] After his denial, when Jesus reinstated Peter, the apostle tried to divert attention to the one disciple who had stayed at the cross – John.[4] Even Paul, though he had accepted his call and was serving God faithfully, still referred to himself as the "worst of sinners".[5] Yet, in each case, as God's calling was finally received and embraced, these servants of God discovered that they had exactly the gifts and abilities they needed. This is why we need these stories – to remind us that when God calls us, God always equips us.

It may be tempting to look at others and compare ourselves unfavorably with them. It may feel like we do not have anything of value to offer to God. But, when we find our place within a Called Community, we discover that we do have something to contribute. We may even discover that talents that we hardly believed were worthy of the name become valuable when they are joined with the gifts of others. As we begin to use our abilities in faith we soon discover what it feels like to be called, and we begin to enjoy the challenges, excitement, anticipation and sense of reward that flow from knowing that we are making a positive difference in the world.

In order to answer God's call we need only to acknowledge

---

[2] Exodus 4:10

[3] Jeremiah 1:6

[4] John 21:20-22

[5] 1 Timothy 1:15

that our gifts – however insignificant they may seem to us – are valuable to God. Then we can learn to make space for the gifts of others. As we embrace our call, in partnership with our companions in the Called Community, we discover that our lives matter. Our names may not resonate around the world, but the contribution we make, when added to the efforts of others seeking to demonstrate God's Reign, certainly does.

to do

Take time to reflect for a moment on your own sense of "giftedness". Think about the things that you are good at, and ask yourself how they can be valuable to the work of God. Notice where God is already using your abilities to touch and serve others, and also take note of any gifts that are not being used.

Now, as you go through today, commit to doing two things. Give thanks for the gifts that God has given you and the opportunities to use your gifts for God's sake. And then, be intentional about making your gifts available to the Called Community to which you belong. This may mean continuing your involvement in some ministry of the church, or it may mean doing something new. Either way, allow your "deep gladness" and the world's "deep need" to meet somewhere in your life.

to pray

Thank you, O God, for calling me and equipping me to contribute to your saving work in the world.

called to worship

...I saw the Lord. He was sitting on a lofty throne, and the train of His robe filled the Temple. – Isaiah 6:1

[I]f we are to find our true identity and our true vocation, we must become 'liturgical', down to the roots of our being.
– Susan J. White

to read

Isaiah 6:1-8

to think about

I had not expected what happened that night. I had been wrestling for the last few weeks with what it meant to believe. The small New Testament that I had received at school from the Gideons had lived in the pocket of my blazer. At the back was a line where I could sign my name to acknowledge that I had received Jesus as my Lord and Savior, but I didn't feel that I was quite ready to make that mark. On the way to church that Sunday evening, I mentioned my struggle to my parents, and they talked me through the basics of faith. In my head it made sense, but I had made commitments before and they had not lasted long. Somehow I knew that I needed more than just a set of ideas in my head.

When I arrived at church and saw who the preacher was,

my heart sank. I knew this retired minister as a sincere follower of Jesus, but the stroke he had suffered years before had left him slow of speech, and, for a fourteen-year-old boy, he was very difficult to listen to. Yet, as he led us through the hymns and prayers, I found myself more engaged than usual. As he preached my mind wandered, but then, as he drew to a close, his words began to capture my attention. I imagined myself in the prison cell he described as he told the story of a murderer who found forgiveness in Christ. Then, as he called the congregation to prayer, and invited us to respond to Jesus, I discovered a deep longing to know this God, not just know about God. The preacher then invited us to look up to Jesus, and I opened my eyes to look at the image of the ascending Christ in the stained glass window. In that moment something began to shift.

After the service, when everyone had moved into the hall for tea, I knelt alone at the communion rail and prayed a simple prayer of commitment, asking God to fill me with God's presence and grace. When I stood up from that rail, I knew that something had changed deep within me, and that I would never be the same person. Within six months I knew that my life would be given over to full-time ministry in God's service. Now, more than thirty years later, I can see how that one, simple act of worship changed the course of my life and made me the person – and the minister – that I am today.

I am not the first to have experienced this kind of transformation in worship. Thousands of years ago, in a time of great turbulence in the land of Israel, an official of the king's court named Isaiah went to the Temple to worship one day. It was an ordinary act in which he would probably have participated regularly, but this day something very different happened. He received a vision of God, and of God's purposes for God's people, that captured his heart. Immediately he faced his own brokenness and cried out in despair, but God's forgiveness and grace touched him. Then, as he heard God's voice calling for a messenger, he could not help but respond. He may have entered the Temple as a politician, but he left it as a prophet.

The act of worship is sometimes seen as an escape from the world and its troubles. We like to think that we can "enter" the presence of God, forget about the world, and get filled by God's presence and Spirit. It's as if our spirituality has become an attempt to separate ourselves from our very real and ordinary humanness, our bodies and minds, our struggles and disappointments. But, this is not how worship is portrayed in the Scriptures. The Bible's worshippers were called to the Tabernacle, or the Temple, or one another's homes, in order to encounter God and be captured by God's dream for the world. They knew that their worship was not an escape from the world, but a place to learn to see the world from God's perspective. They fully expected, when the worship gathering ended, to be sent back out to engage more deeply in the daily task of being fully whole, fully human, and fully immersed in the work of healing and liberating others.

This is why every worship gathering begins with a *call to worship*. This small but significant practice is not just a precursor to singing a few songs and praying a few prayers. It's not even just an invitation to meet with God. It is a symbolic act in which we recognize that, as followers of Christ, we are *Called People* who participate in a *Called Community*. We hear the call to worship as a call to action – a moment in which we gather to remember our mission and our purpose, and to receive our instructions and training for living out the call through the coming week. James Smith describes this call to worship in this way:

> So this is not just a call to do something "religious," something to be merely added to our "normal" life. It is a call to be(come) *human*, to take up the vocation of being fully and authentically human, and to be a community and people who image God to the world.[1]

When we hear the call to worship we are faced with the choice either to respond or to hold ourselves back. If we decide to respond, we do so bringing our whole attention,

---

[1] Smith, James K. A., *Desiring the Kingdom – Worship, Worldview and Cultural Formation,* (Grand Rapids, Baker Academic, 2009), 162-163.

energy and participation into the worship that follows. We respond knowing that the practices and rituals, the stories and vocabulary of our liturgy will change us. Our lives will be reshaped to reflect the attitudes and purposes of Jesus. In answering the call to worship we open ourselves to this transformation willingly and gladly.

To be called to worship is not to disappear into a church building where we can find safety among people who think and look like us. It is to take the dangerous step into an encounter with God that will radically change how we live and who we are. To respond to the call to worship is to accept God's agenda for our lives, and to be recruited as participants in making God's Reign visible in our world.

to ϑo

Go back and reread the Isaiah passage. Notice how the praise of the seraphim opened Isaiah to this encounter with God, and created the environment in which he could hear and answer God's call. Take a moment to reflect on your experience of God. Give praise for the various aspects of God's nature that strengthen and inspire you. Keep up this attitude of praise throughout the day, and, as you do, listen for the call of God in each moment.

to pray

For your Reign of love and justice I praise you, O God, and for calling me to be part of it.

day fourteen

Living a Called Life

Remember, dear brothers and sisters, that few of you were wise in the world's eyes or powerful or wealthy when God called you. – 1 Corinthians 1:26

Few of us can do great things, but all of us can do small things with great love. – Mother Teresa

to read
1 Corinthians 1:25-31

to think about

It had been twenty years, but as we shared lunch with this couple who had been such good friends, it felt like we were right back at university. We reminisced about our time together on the Student Christian Association committee, and our mission trip to help build a small church just outside of Butterworth in what was then known as the Transkei. We had gone our separate ways when we had finished our studies, but now they had returned to South Africa after a long time in England, and we had reconnected with amazing ease and comfort.

As I reflected on our time together, I realized that the thread that keeps me connected with many of my university friends is the partnership we shared in various projects, groups or tasks. The relationships we formed as we worked together, played together and dreamed together have endured through the years, in spite of long separations and huge distances. The belonging we found was deep and life-changing, and it has been a gift I have carried with me through my life.

As a group of young students we had somehow realized that we were all called by God to live with purpose and to make a contribution. We had believed that we could live that call immediately, without waiting to finish our studies or be ordained in our churches. Together we had sought to embody the mission of Jesus right where we were, in our daily activities and relationships. The result was that we had found ourselves working in hospitals, schools, homes for seniors and for people with mental and physical disabilities. We had boldly gone into the townships of Grahamstown to worship with people from whom the apartheid law of the day had tried to separate us. And we had discovered life – rich, full, connected and deeply meaningful. Together we had learned to belong and make a contribution to our world by embracing the call of Jesus to "follow me".

It is tempting to look back at the first century church with the belief that this community was special. Their leaders had known Jesus and heard his teaching first hand. They were all filled with passion and, as a persecuted community, they needed to be strongly committed to one another. We may feel that, in our time, we cannot hope to make the kind of difference to the world that these uniquely powerful believers did. But, the apostle Paul gives us a glimpse into this early church that reveals how very like us they were.

The church in Corinth, for example, was known for its factions and leadership struggles,[1] the selfishness and lack of consideration among some of its members,[2] and its rather overzealous emotionalism.[3] Yet, at the start of his letter, Paul

---

[1] 1 Corinthians 1:11-13

[2] 1 Corinthians 11:20-22

[3] 1 Corinthians 14:26-33

affirms that they are called by God. They are participants in God's "foolish" plan of salvation, in spite of the fact that few of them were prominent, wealthy or gifted. These early Christians were ordinary people like us. They made mistakes like us, and they quarreled with one another like us. Yet, as they attempted each day to live out their calling in Christ, they changed the world forever.

When we hear the call to worship we cannot help but realize that God is invested in us. Our lives matter in God's "foolish" plan to bring the world into wholeness and unity in Christ. We are called not just to participate in a time of worship on Sundays, not just to wait for a future life in heavenly glory, but to live the mission of Christ every day of our lives.

As we gather for worship, we come as Called Ones who are part of a Called Community. We come to learn, a little more each week, about the nature of this call and our part in it. In the liturgy we learn that every action, every word, every moment and every interaction has value for God's mission if it is filled with the spirit of worship and done in the love of Christ. We also discover that God's call connects us. We find a place of belonging in the Called Community, where we can add our contribution to those of others, and make a far greater difference in the world than we could alone. We discover a new connectedness with our neighbors as we learn to recognize opportunities to serve and love them. And we discover a new sense of being at home in this world that God loves so much, and for which we are called to care.

Living as followers of Christ and proclaimers of God's Reign does not necessarily mean that we have to give up our jobs and become ordained ministers or missionaries. For most of us, following the call of God does not mean doing great things at all. It means doing small things with great love, as Mother Teresa put it. It means doing everything with the attitude that we do it for God.[4] And it means making God's Reign the focal point around which we orient our lives, and by which we

---

[4] Colossians 3:23

make every decision. All we have to do to find this life of purpose, meaning, joy and belonging is answer the call to worship, and then allow our worship to teach us how to live out God's call from moment to moment.

to ꝺo

Set aside some time today to consider God's call on your life. Begin by sitting in silence. You may want to close your eyes and deepen your breathing. Then allow your mind to explore what God's call might mean for you. Remember times when you have been able to make a contribution to others. How did that feel for you? Think about the gifts you have to offer, and how they can be used by God. Be honest about your fears and doubts, and take note of what it might cost you to answer God's call.

Then, if you can – and only as far as you are able in this moment – commit to living as one of God's Called Ones. Don't worry about the specifics. As you offer yourself to God, you will be led into service in God's way and God's time. Finish by giving thanks for God's investment in your life, and then seek to live each moment of this day with a sense of purpose.

to pray

As you have invested yourself in me, O God, I now commit to live as one of your Called Ones, in Jesus' name.

to explore together

ICE BREAKER

When have you felt like you had a strong sense of purpose? How did this affect you?

WORSHIP

Begin by inviting the group to share areas in their life where they feel called – whether it's to parenthood, a particular job or ministry, or a specific task. Then offer prayers of praise and thanksgiving for God's invitation to be part of God's work in the world.

Take a moment in silence where each person can reflect on areas where he or she has resisted God's call, and invite short prayers of confession. Then, moving into pairs, share your experience of God's call and pray for one another as you seek to follow God's purpose in your lives.

Close by singing or reading a hymn of commitment.

READING

Ephesians 4:1-7

DISCUSSION QUESTIONS

1. What stood out for you in this week's reflections?
2. How do you feel about the idea that you are called by God? How does this make you feel more at home in the world?
3. How has God already equipped you and given you a "special gift" (Ephesians 4:7) for the work God has called you to do?
4. How does the call to worship teach you to live as a called person?
5. How can you commit a little more to living a called life?

week three

invocation

Come close to God, and God will come close to you.
– James 4:8a

You basically don't belong in the universe until you are connected to the centre and the whole, and a word for that is "God".
– Richard Rohr

thought for the week

"We are living in a world that is absolutely transparent, and God is shining through it all the time...The only thing is that we don't see it."[1] This quote, from Trappist monk Thomas Merton, reveals a tragic truth, and an exciting opportunity, in our living. With the growth of rational, scientific inquiry, many of the world's mysteries have become mysteries no more. We can now understand and control the world as never before. But, for too many of us, we have limited the world to what we can perceive and understand. Even for people of faith, the world is primarily engaged through our senses and our intellect. The realm of Spirit has largely been relegated to a different time and place – an other-worldly dimension which we hope to enjoy some time after we die, but which has little bearing on how we live or think now.

Yet, as we seek to live as those who are called, we quickly realize that our natural abilities are insufficient. We need resources beyond ourselves, and we need to see and understand with divine wisdom.

It is because of this universal human need for direct connection with God that our worship includes, among the first of its practices, the *invocation*. One of the meanings of the word "invoke" is to "call on". As we gather in worship we invoke God's presence and Spirit. As we hear God's call on our lives, so we respond by calling on God to make God's presence known to us, and to fill us with God's Spirit. We open ourselves to receive God's wisdom, strength and perspective to guide us in our following of Jesus. This simple but profound act changes how we live, and teaches us that we are empowered by God, and are always at home in God's presence and God's world.

---

[1] Thomas Merton, from an audiotape made in 1965, quoted by Marcus Borg in *The Heart of Christianity,* (HarperSanFrancisco, 2003), 155.

day fifteen

a divided world

---

*A man named Ananias lived there. He was a godly man,
deeply devoted to the law, and well regarded by all the Jews of
Damascus. He came and stood beside me and said, 'Brother
Saul, regain your sight.' And that very moment I could see him!
Then he told me, 'The God of our ancestors has chosen you to
know His will and to see the Righteous One and hear Him
speak.' – Acts 22:12-14*

*We don't see things as they are, we see things as we are.
– Anais Nin*

to read

Acts 22:1-16

to think about

"John!"

My head spun as I tried to check my mirrors and the road
around me all at once. My feet hovered over the brake, my
hands tightened on the steering wheel, and I braced myself for
the impact that I thought was imminent. Then, with a gleeful
smile, Debbie pointed out the window at the flowers blooming
at the side of the road. "Look," she laughed, "daffodils!"

As a relatively new driver, who, for months, had navigated
nothing more difficult than the quiet roads of our university
town of Grahamstown, I was nervous as we made our way on
to the busy streets of Port Elizabeth. We had not timed our

journey well, and so we entered the city at rush hour. With my focus fixed on the task of driving, my brain had completely filtered out the daffodils, but, with her attention free to wander, Debbie had filtered out the traffic. In her love for all growing things, she had been unable to contain her exclamation of delight when she saw the bright yellows of one her favorite floral friends.

Our minds make these kinds of "filtering decisions" constantly. As information comes into our brains through our senses, we all receive it and process it differently. Our "filters" are shaped by our age, gender, race, language, culture, religion and a host of other influences, which means that we actually all live in very different worlds.

The apostle Paul, who had lived his life according to the rigid filters of the Hebrew law, suddenly had his entire perspective of the world changed as he encountered Jesus on the road to Damascus. He had been convinced that the followers of Jesus were blasphemers who sought to undermine the ancient truths of his faith. He had believed that the only appropriate response was to arrest and punish these heretics before they could do any lasting damage to the religion that he loved. His world was clear and defined, and the law gave him a comforting sense of security and identity. But then, in the middle of his quest to wipe out this new movement, his entire world was reshaped. His encounter with Jesus changed his convictions and his behavior, transforming him from a persecutor to an evangelist.

Years later, Paul returned to Jerusalem from his missionary travels in spite of being warned to stay away. As a result of his new faith, and his friendship with Gentiles, Paul's presence in the Temple caused a riot, and he was arrested. In Acts 22, the apostle addressed his opponents and shared the story of his conversion. Unfortunately, though, his hearers had not shared his experience of Christ, and so they were unable to accept his view of the world. He remained in chains and was taken to Rome to stand trial. Paul's story reveals how powerfully our unique perspectives of the world impact even our faith. As with the disciples and their persecutors, our understandings of God, and of how the Creator interacts with creation, are subject to our brains' "filtering decisions". This is why it often takes some dramatic new experience or insight to change what we believe and how we live.

Human history tells the stories of many such radical shifts of understanding that brought about a whole new way of living – for better or worse. For example, in the pre-modern age, the world was viewed as mysterious, magical and filled with supernatural beings who would bless or curse at whim. Disease and natural disasters were believed to be the punishment of the gods, while health and good harvests were signs of God's blessing. When the Enlightenment came along, science and philosophy found reasonable explanations for many natural processes, and the old, magical ideas fell away.

An unexpected by-product of this scientific worldview, is the separation of the "physical" realm and the "spiritual". In an attempt to live with intellectual integrity, many of us have allowed science to define our world in measurable, material terms. We have pushed God into the "gaps" where science has either no interest or insufficient data. This has led to the creation of divided people with a divided view of the world. We live in the body, but believe that our physical experiences are not really part of our true, spiritual nature. We view God as apart from us, living in some heaven "out there", and needing to be petitioned to "intervene" in our lives. As a result we can easily end up feeling homeless and at odds with the material world.

Having lost the sense that our bodies are sacred, we feel disconnected from its needs and drives. Consequently, we too easily fall into addiction (to overeating, sex, substances, lethargy) or asceticism (denying our legitimate needs in an attempt to keep ourselves "pure"). Having lost the sense that the earth is sacred, we too easily abuse it as nothing more than a storehouse of natural resources from which we can enrich ourselves. The devastating effects of our divided lives are seen in violence and war, in the spread of sexually-transmitted diseases, in human trafficking for sex, in the global epidemic of obesity and "lifestyle" diseases, and in the changing climate of the earth.

What we need is to realize that this divided view of ourselves and our world is just a "filter". It is not the way things are, it is just the way we see them. And we need to open ourselves to a dramatic new encounter – of the magnitude of a Damascus road – with the unity and sacredness of our lives and our world.

to do

Reflect on your life over the last few weeks. Where do you see evidence of a divided view of the world? Have you had any moments when you have viewed your body as unimportant or even evil? Have you been tempted to ignore the impact that your life has on the planet? Have you found yourself longing for a heaven that is free from the body and its struggles? How has this way of seeing the world impacted you, and those around you? Take a moment to confess this to God, and ask for God to forgive and change you.

As you go through today, try to notice any time when you are tempted to separate the "spiritual" from the "physical" in your mind. Then, try to recognize the unity and connectedness of the world.

to pray

Forgive me when I see you as distant, O God, and when I live as if your created world does not matter.

day sixteen

god in creation

Then Jacob awoke from his sleep and said, "Surely the LORD is in this place, and I wasn't even aware of it!" – Genesis 28:16

There is a communion with God, and a communion with the earth, and a communion with God through the earth.
– Pierre Teilhard de Chardin

to read
Genesis 28:10-19

to think about
Pierre Teilhard de Chardin's first memory was as a five- or six-year-old boy, when he held a piece of hair, freshly cut from his head by his mother, up to the fire. It was consumed in an instant and he was consumed by a sudden terror. For the first time he had encountered his own frailty. As he grew, his concern about the fragility of all things was tempered by the influence of both of his parents. From his mother he learned a deep Christian spirituality. From his father, he received a love for the natural world, and a keen skill for observation. At boarding school his spirituality was further nurtured to the point where he decided to become a Jesuit.

His training in the order encouraged both his theological development, and his study of science. When, in 1905, he was sent to Cairo to do a teaching internship, he had the opportunity to explore the Egyptian countryside, where he studied the local flora and fossils. A few years later, while completing his theological studies in England, Teilhard encountered *Creative Evolution*, a newly published book by Henri Bergson that challenged the idea of the separation of spirit and matter. From this time on, the course of Teilhard's life was set, as he brought together his deep spirituality and his thorough scientific inquiry.

He went on to study paleontology and geology, and to travel the world, including many years in exile in China as a result of religious opposition to his work. Although his church refused permission for much of his writing to be published, after his death in 1955, there was no longer any way to prevent it.[1] Since then, Teilhard's thought has inspired scientists and theologians, and has continued to make significant contributions to the dialogue between science and faith. For Pierre Teilhard de Chardin, there was no contradiction between his spirituality and his scientific inquiry. On the contrary, as he studied the world, he found God's fingerprints everywhere, and he taught others the valuable truth that the Creator can be encountered *within* creation.

Thousands of years before Teilhard wrote of his discoveries, a man by the name of Jacob encountered God in a similarly life-changing way. On the run from his brother Esau, whom he had cheated, he stopped in a field to rest overnight. As he slept, he had a vision of a ladder stretching up to heaven with angels moving up and down on it. At the top of the ladder he saw God, who promised to protect him, and to give him land and descendants. When Jacob awoke he was amazed and exclaimed, "God is in this place – truly. And I didn't even know it!"[2]

This same truth is echoed throughout the Bible. The prophet Jeremiah proclaims: "Can anyone hide from me in a

---

[1] A far more detailed account of Pierre Teilhard de Chardin's life can be found at: http://www.teilharddechardin.org/biography.html (accessed 19 September 2012)

[2] Genesis 28:16 (The Message)

secret place? Am I not everywhere in all the heavens and earth?" says the Lord.[3] The Psalmist writes:

> I can never escape from Your Spirit! I can never get away from Your presence! If I go up to heaven, You are there; if I go down to the grave, You are there. If I ride the wings of the morning, if I dwell by the farthest oceans, even there Your hand will guide me, and Your strength will support me.[4]

The New Testament also affirms the unity between God and creation. Jesus, in his conversation with the Samaritan woman at the well, confidently asserts that worship requires no specific temple or geographic place. Rather, we can encounter God everywhere as we worship in "spirit and truth".[5] This is why Jesus describes the Reign of God as something we know within us and among us,[6] and why Paul refers to us, both individually and collectively, as temples of the Holy Spirit.[7]

It is neither good science nor good faith to create a separation between the spiritual and physical realms. The divided view of the world is not a biblical view, and it does not lead us to wholeness and a sense of belonging. When spirit and matter are separate, we cannot feel at home in our bodies or in this world, because we believe that they are both temporary and will be destroyed. But, when we allow the Scriptures to open our eyes and hearts to the Spirit that sustains and moves through creation, our whole experience of life is empowered and enriched. When we know that God is immersed in the universe that God made, we learn to see the world as sacred – of infinite, eternal value. When we know that the world is not just a temporary waiting place, but part of God's eternal creation, we stop feeling like strangers on this planet, and discover that we are truly at home here. When we

---

[3] Jeremiah 23:24

[4] Psalm 139:7-10

[5] See John 4:20-24

[6] Luke 17:21

[7] See 1 Corinthians 3:16 and 1 Corinthians 6:19

recognize that God's Spirit lives within us, that God's Reign can be established in our hearts, and that even our bodies are part of God's plan of salvation, we discover a new, eternal value to our lives. To embrace this vision of a united cosmos is a powerful and life-giving experience – and it can be yours right now, if you are ready to receive it.

to ðo

Take a moment to think of a song or hymn that expresses the beauty of creation. As you reflect on the words, try to remember any time when you have been awestruck by the glory of the world around you. Have these moments given you a deeper sense of God's presence? Have you felt more "at home" in the world at these times?

Now offer a prayer of praise for creation, and for the God who fills it. As you pray, open yourself to God's presence, and allow yourself to feel the connection between the spiritual and physical realities. As you go into your day, try to maintain this attitude of praise, and seek to increase your awareness of God's presence in each moment and place.

to pray

I praise you, O God, for the world you made, and that I can encounter you in it.

day seventeen

god in the flesh

Then [Jesus] said to Thomas, "Put your finger here, and look at My hands. Put your hand into the wound in My side. Don't be faithless any longer. Believe!" "My Lord and my God!" Thomas exclaimed. – John 20:27-28

God, who knows no boundaries took on the shocking confines of a baby's skin… – Philip Yancey

to read

John 20:24-31

to think about

The procession always ended at the small mud hut where the missionaries lived. Every year, on Christmas Sunday morning, the people of the little village in what is now the Democratic Republic of Congo, would wake early to climb the nearby mountain. As the sun rose, they would gather flowers and then return to the village in a procession singing Christmas carols. When they reached the home of the missionary family, they would form a swaying, musical circle around the hut in celebration of the birth of Christ. Although the son of the missionary couple was just a little boy – younger than seven years old – the memory of these processions remained in his heart throughout his life. Perhaps it is not surprising, then, that Dr Robert Webber went on to become a well-respected theologian whose teaching inspired and renewed thousands of churches until his death in 2007, and whose books continue to shape the worship life of churches across the globe.[1]

Two millennia after the birth of Jesus, people from small villages in rural Africa, and people from the big cities in Europe and the Americas continue to celebrate that it happened. In countries where religion can be practiced freely, and in places where the profession of faith can mean death, followers of Christ continue to remember this one significant life. The Christian faith, in its entirety, rests on a single, radical idea, which is reflected in the early morning procession of the Congolese worshippers: God has become known through a physical human being, at a specific point in human history. In spite of war and revolution, poverty and disease, climate change and inequality, the incarnation of God in Christ remains the sustaining power for people of faith across the globe.

Today the idea has become so common that the word "incarnation" is often part of ordinary conversation. It's easy to forget that when Jesus walked the earth, the Jews considered it blasphemy to claim that any human being was God, and the Romans considered it treason to worship any person other than Caesar. Either way, to proclaim a belief in the incarnation meant certain death.

Perhaps that's why, when he returned to the other disciples, Thomas was reluctant to just accept their stories of resurrection. If he was going to stake his life on his faith, he needed to know for himself that it was true. As a consequence of this caution history has left Thomas with the unflattering nickname of "Doubter". If you follow his story, though, no label could be more inappropriate. When Jesus suggested returning to Judea after hearing about Lazarus' death, the disciples tried to dissuade him because of the threats against his life. But, Thomas had a different response. "Let's go too," he said, "and die with Jesus."[2]   After his encounter with

---

[1] This story is related in Dr. Webber's book *Worship is a Verb*, (Peabody, Massachusetts, Hendrickson Publishers, 1992), 22.

[2] John 11:16

Christ, Thomas became a passionate evangelist, traveling as far as India, and ultimately dying a martyr's death for his faith. He wanted to be certain of the resurrection, and of the shocking truth that it proclaimed before he committed himself. But once he had encountered the risen Jesus, he immediately accepted that this man was also God.[3]

We will never really know the mechanics of how God became human in Jesus, but if we choose to believe, it impacts every facet of our lives. It is impossible to accept the incarnation and still see God and creation as separate. If the incarnation tells us anything, it is that the physical and spiritual worlds are indivisible. Matter and spirit are equally valuable to God, and both are necessary for the life of human beings and of the cosmos.

But the incarnation was never meant to be a once-off event, that involved only one unique human being. In biblical language, Jesus is the "firstborn"[4] – the primary and unique incarnation. But, the Bible invites us to recognize that God's Spirit resides within us and within all things, and so we are all, individually and together, "little incarnations". This is what Paul had in mind, I believe, when he proclaimed to the people of Athens that "in [God] we live and move and exist",[5] and when he wrote to the Ephesian Church that "There is one...God and Father, who is over all and in all and living through all".[6]

When we begin to take incarnation seriously, everything begins to change. The old, divided view of the world falls away, along with the sense of disconnectedness that we once knew, and a new way of seeing takes its place. We learn to recognize the sacred presence of God permeating the cosmos and our own lives, and we discover that we truly do belong in this amazing, sacred world.

---

[3] John 20:28

[4] Romans 8:29

[5] Acts 17:28

[6] Ephesians 4:5,6

We also discover a new hope for the future. Like Jesus, we are incarnations in which God's Spirit lives, and, like Jesus, we look forward to being resurrected. The Bible promises that we will all be raised from death to live in a new body[7] on a new, resurrected earth.[8] It is not just our spirits that are eternal, but our entire being, including our bodies, minds and souls. When this truth has captured our hearts, we are no longer at war with our own flesh, and we can finally, eternally, be at home.

to do

Sit in silence for a moment, and allow your mind to explore the idea of incarnation. Allow any questions or struggles to arise, but don't get caught up in trying to find answers (you can do that another time if you want). Think about Jesus and what it means for you that he was God in the flesh. Now think about yourself, and become aware of God's Spirit moving around you and within you. Once you have allowed this sense of being a "little incarnation" to settle inside you, respond with a prayer of thanksgiving. Try to carry this thankfulness through the day.

to pray

For becoming flesh and for filling the world – and me – with your Spirit, I give thanks, O God.

---

[7] 1 Corinthians 15:1-24

[8] 2 Peter 3:13; Isaiah 65:17; Revelation 21:1-5

day eighteen

filled with spirit

---

*If you love Me, obey My commandments. And I will ask the
Father, and He will give you another Advocate, who will never
leave you.*
– John 14:15-16

*Who is the Holy Spirit? The Holy Spirit is the Burning Spirit. It
kindles the hearts of humankind. Like tympanum and lyre it
plays them, gathering volume in the temple of the soul...*
*The Holy Spirit is the life of the life of all creatures...that gives
existence to all form...*
The Holy Spirit resurrects and awakens everything that is.
– Hildegard of Bingen

to read

John 14:15-18, 26-27

to think about

"I felt so in need of real worship that it felt like a thirst." It
was not that worship wasn't happening. On the contrary, in
the few days prior to reaching this dry and desperate place,
Kathleen Norris had shared in worship a number of times.
Worship was a regular feature on the program of the
conference she was attending. The problem was that the
liturgy felt more like a workshop, with every hymn and prayer
chosen for some instructional purpose. When, in one of the
group discussions, she mentioned the value of visiting other

churches in order to have a different *experience* of worship, she was dismissed, and the group leader quickly moved on.

Finally, longing for some refreshment for her soul, she called the local Dominican priory and joined them in worship the next day. The aesthetics and "polish" of the service were nowhere near the standard of the conference she had left, but she "wanted worship with room for the Holy Spirit," and there, among a ragtag group of strangers, she found it – an encounter with the real, living presence of God.[1]

This same thirst has been felt by human beings throughout the ages – not least by a group of nervous Christ-followers who were learning that their Master was about to leave them. In the last few hours he shared with his disciples, Jesus tried to prepare them for what was to come. As they gathered to share a meal, Jesus washed the disciples' feet, explaining that, as he had served them, so they should serve and love one another. Then he began to talk about the time when he would no longer be with them. He was leaving, he explained, but another *Paraclete* – one who would be alongside them – would come. This Holy Spirit would be like having Jesus with them, but in a different way. They already knew this Spirit, he assured them, but in time they would be "filled", and then, the Spirit would teach them, lead them and empower them.

A few weeks later, on the day of Pentecost, as the frightened disciples huddled together in an upstairs room still trying to process Jesus' death, resurrection and mysterious ascension, their entire world changed. They heard a strong wind, saw what looked like flames on one another's heads, and found themselves unable to contain their joy as they experienced God's presence in an amazingly immediate and powerful way. They found themselves rushing out into the streets where people from all over the world understood what they were saying, in spite of language differences.

---

[1] This story is told in the chapter entitled *Worship*, from Kathleen Norris's book, *Amazing Grace: A Vocabulary of Faith,* (New York, Riverhead Books, 1998), 246-250.

From that day on, their lives were filled with a constant sense of God's presence. They knew a confidence that they had never had before, and they found themselves sharing the news of God's Reign boldly and fearlessly. But, what made their influence so dramatic was that they invited anyone who would respond to receive this same gift. God's Spirit was available to all, they proclaimed, and the dramatic experiences of those who believed them proved their words to be true.[2]

The Pentecost experience often raises more questions than it answers. It can be challenging to understand what the Bible means when it speaks of "being filled" with the Spirit. Many attempts to explain this event either tend to create a sort of "spiritual hierarchy" between those who are filled and those who aren't, or rationalize the experience so much that it loses its power. We must be careful not to allow our need for explanations to limit the movement of God's Spirit. One thing is sure, though: human beings long for more than just knowledge *about* God. We yearn, like Kathleen Norris, to *experience* the *reality* of God. This is why it is so comforting to know that the promise of Jesus, experienced by the disciples at Pentecost, is available to every one of us.

I don't believe for a moment that there is any person or place where God's Spirit is not already present. I do believe, however, that we often go through our daily routines completely unaware of the Spirit's activity and power. God's Spirit was already moving on the earth before the day of Pentecost, but on that day a new awareness, a new ability to perceive and experience God, was awakened in the human soul. Now, in order to know the reality of God in our own lives, we need only ask.

The apostle Paul loves to speak of the Christian life as living "in Christ" and as having Christ "in us".[3] Imagine throwing an empty bottle into a lake. As the water floods the bottle, it sinks into the depths. The water is in the bottle, and

---

[2] The biblical account of this experience is found in Acts 2. The rest of the book of Acts tells the story of what happened as a result. It's amazing and inspiring reading!

[3] Romans 8 is just one example of this.

the bottle is in the water. In the same way, God longs for us to live with a constant sense of being in God's presence, and of having God's presence and power within us, flooding into every aspect of our lives.

The experience of being filled with God's Spirit is not about becoming "more spiritual" or "other-worldly". It's not about trying to escape the struggles of our human existence. It's about discovering what it means to be fully human in the way God created us to be – in union with God. It's about realizing that we can be "little incarnations" – flesh and blood filled with God's Spirit – and living from that awareness every day. It's about finally knowing, in the deepest parts of ourselves, that we have a home in God's presence, and God has made God's home within us.

to ᵭo

Deepen your breathing and relax your body until you feel at rest. Then, in whatever way you feel comfortable, open yourself to God. Invite God's Spirit to fill you. Try to release any attempts to analyze your experience, and let go of any specific expectations you may have. Simply open yourself to whatever may come. Stay in this attitude of openness for as long as you need. Then move into your day with a commitment to remain open to the presence and activity of God's Spirit in your life.

to pray

Come, Holy Spirit; fill me with your presence and power.

day nineteen

invocation

Then Elisha prayed, "O LORD, open his eyes and let him see!"
The LORD opened the young man's eyes, and when he looked
up, he saw that the hillside around Elisha was filled with
horses and chariots of fire. – 2 Kings 6:17

Worship is an act of attention to the living God who rules,
speaks and reveals, creates and redeems, orders and
blesses...Failure to worship consigns us to a life of spasms and
jerks, at the mercy of every advertisement, every seduction,
every siren. – Eugene H. Peterson

to read
2 Kings 6:8-23

to think about

"When I'm out on the water, I often see dolphins swimming right beside me and sharks deep beneath my kayak. At these moments I feel closer to God than I ever do in church."

These words were spoken by a friend of mine who has been a faithful worshiper for many years. As I thought about his words, I had to acknowledge that I often feel the same way when I hike through the mountains in and around Cape Town. But I also realized that there is a reason I am able to be so aware of God's presence outside of the church.

"How did you learn to recognize God in the sea and the dolphin?" I asked my friend. "Could it have been your worship that has opened your awareness?" He nodded silently for a while and then quietly remarked that for him this was a new way of looking at worship.

I suspect that his wrestling is shared by many people both in our churches and outside of them. It is unfortunate that worship has come to be seen as a self-contained activity that is an end in itself. What we do on Sunday is too often seen as a withdrawal from the world into a different reality in which we "meet with God" for a time in order to "be filled" before returning to the business of living each day. But, the value of our worship gatherings is not in what happens in church. Worship is significant because of the way it changes how we see and experience every day and every situation. Worship is where we learn to recognize God's presence and activity so that we can live with an awareness of God in any place or time.

In the Old Testament book of 2 Kings, the prophet Elisha had learned to recognize God's activity, to hear God's voice and see God's presence throughout the world. So attuned was he to God, the Scriptures say, that he could predict the movements of enemy troops and report this to his king, saving the lives of many soldiers in the process. Needless to say the enemies of Israel were unimpressed, and so the king of Aram sent an army to kidnap the prophet.

One morning, when Elisha's servant went outside, he was greeted with the fearsome sight of a massive military force surrounding the house. When he reported this to his Master, Elisha was calm, and explained that the army on their side was much larger than the one that had come to capture him. The servant must have thought the prophet had lost his mind, since he could see no friendly troops. But when Elisha prayed for God to open his eyes, he suddenly became aware of a massive detachment of flaming chariots. Once he had learned to see, the world became a different place for this young man.

Throughout the history of the church, worship gatherings have included a moment of *invocation*. Placed within the first few minutes of the liturgy, the invocation is like Elisha's prayer for the eyes of his servant to be opened. It is the moment in which we ask God to make us aware of God's Spirit moving within us and among us. It is a moment of learning to recognize the presence, the voice and the activity of God in our lives.

This act of opening ourselves to God's Spirit, becomes the key to living each day with an abiding sense of God's presence. The worship service becomes the classroom in which we school our hearts and minds to be aware of God's Spirit and God's activity in every moment, every situation and every interaction. In addition, we learn to see God's presence as an invitation. We learn that God is always making the first move to connect with us, and we discover that we need only respond in order to know deep, intimate union with God.

As we gather, free for a brief time from the distractions of cellphones, business and responsibility, we are able to experience a "little Pentecost" – a "little outpouring" of God's Spirit. Our worship opens us to a real *experience* of God, and we discover what it means to live under the teaching and guidance of the Spirit. As we respond to the Spirit's promptings in worship, so we train our hearts to respond whenever the Spirit nudges us in our daily lives. As we allow ourselves to be "filled" with God's Spirit, so we train ourselves to draw on God's power for every challenge we may face through the week.

The prayer of invocation is both a practice of learning to see the world as filled with God, and of learning to be open to God's work in our own lives. This means that we can pray invocation prayers all the time. Worship teaches us that we are always able to open ourselves to the Spirit, and that the Spirit is always available to us. As Jesus taught in the Sermon on the Mount:

> And so I tell you, keep on asking, and you will receive what you ask for. Keep on seeking, and you will find. Keep on knocking, and the door will be opened to you...
> If you sinful people know how to give good gifts to your

children, how much more will your heavenly Father give
the Holy Spirit to those who ask Him."[1]

When we allow our prayers of invocation to do their work,
we experience the world in much the same way as the Irish
saint Patrick did:

Christ be with me, Christ within me,
Christ behind me, Christ before me,
Christ beside me, Christ to win me,
Christ to comfort and restore me.[2]

to ðo

Create a time and space to be free from distractions. Allow
your mind to wander as you allow your feelings about the
world, and your place in it, to surface. Now, picture God's
Spirit moving through you and through the earth. You can
use one of the biblical metaphors like water, air or light, or
allow your own image of the Spirit to guide you. Now, spend
time praying for God to open your eyes to the Spirit's presence
in and around you. Keep this prayer in your heart as you go
through your day.

to pray

May I, and all people, learn to recognize your Spirit's
presence and power in our world, O God.

---

[1] Luke 11:9,13

[2] This is a small excerpt from a much larger prayer known as St.
Patrick's Breastplate. To read the full version, see this Wikipedia
article, which also gives some of the history and usage of St. Patrick's
Breastplate in worship: http://en.wikipedia.org/wiki/
Saint_Patrick's_Breastplate.

day twenty

at home in god's presence

But how can we sing the songs of the LORD while in a pagan land? – Psalms 137:4

Unless we also carry within our hearts the God whom we are seeking, we will never find God. – Esther de Waal

to read

Psalm 137

to think about

It takes a lot of anger and pain, and a very small sense of God, to pray that babies would be smashed against rocks. The people of Israel had, through many centuries, experienced deep pain and desperate disappointment. The once glorious kingdom of David had, under his grandchildren, become divided. The fortunes of the people had bounced from prosperity to oppression, depending on the character of their leaders. Finally they had been conquered by pagan nations and carried into exile. The Temple in Jerusalem, the place where they believed God dwelt, had been reduced to ruins, and the chosen nation was devastated.

But, the music of the Temple had been famous for its beauty, and so the Babylonian captors asked to hear it. The best the exiles could do was to lament their inability to sing

God's songs in this pagan land. From their perspective the destruction of the Temple could only mean that God had abandoned them, and they were now vulnerable and alone. Everything they had known and loved was gone, but they were determined to cling to their memories and nurse their grudges. That was all they had left, and it had made them murderously angry against those who had conquered them.

It is an unfortunate reality in our world that fear, humiliation and pain often generate this kind of violence. As we become increasingly self-protective, our view of God becomes smaller and more exclusive, and we find ourselves able to justify our worst motives and behaviors in God's name. As Lauren Artress writes:

> As fear for our individual as well as collective future increases, the flight into a literal interpretation of the Bible is experiencing a dramatic revival. This fear breeds small-mindedness and mean-spiritedness. The tyranny of the letter of the law...is overshadowing the spirit of love that was intended by the law of the Divine.[1]

The great tragedy of this crisis is that it is completely unnecessary. If the people of Israel had taken a moment to look beyond their despair, they would have seen that God had not abandoned them. They would have learned that God was just as close to them in Babylon as God had ever been in Israel, and they would have been able to draw comfort and strength from singing God's song among their pagan captors. Instead of feeling dislocated, they could have learned to be at home even in this strange, foreign land.

For followers of Christ it is tempting to adopt the same fearful, self-protective attitude. It is easy to fall into believing that God is "with us" on "our side" and that God is not with others who believe and act differently from us. It is tempting to live with a kind of spiritual dislocation, feeling homeless in this world as we long for our "home in heaven". But, to live like this is to risk becoming small-minded and mean-spirited.

---

[1] Artress, Lauren, *Walking A Sacred Path: Rediscovering the Labyrinth as a Spiritual Tool,* (New York, Riverhead Books, 1995), 8.

It is to risk finding comfortable justifications for our most hate-filled and violent tendencies. It is to deny the reality that God's Spirit fills the earth, and that we can always be at home when we learn to be aware of God's presence within and around us.

The call to be at home in God's presence is not just about facing the great crises of our world. It is just as much about learning to discover the sacredness of every moment and every place. When our lives are flooded with a sense of God, wherever we are becomes holy ground, pregnant with the potential for a true encounter with God's Spirit.

A friend and colleague of mine recently shared an experience of discovering unexpected beauty and sacredness while on a shopping trip. As he confronted his usual boredom, he decided to turn the supermarket into an art exhibition. While placing groceries into his cart, he used the camera on his cell phone to capture images of ordinary things that, when viewed carefully and mindfully, became extraordinarily beautiful. The result was that an activity that was normally unpleasant became exciting and soul-nourishing. In conversation with him on his blog he made the following, revealing comment: "The experience of the sacred has become very wide for me."[2]

When we allow our worship, and our experience of God, to teach us to live "in the Spirit" like this, we discover that our true home is not in a place, but in our connections with God and with one another. When we are aware of God's presence at every time and in every situation, and when we allow our lives to be shaped and directed by God's love, we discover that we belong, wherever we may be. Even in the most painful and difficult circumstances we are able to lean into the sense of security, comfort and protection that we find in God's presence. Though we may still have to face tragedies and traumas, we will do so as children of God who know that they

---

[2] To read the blog post and see some of the photos he took that day, go to his Candid Impressions blog: http:// candidpresence.wordpress.com/2012/06/23/the-supermarket-as-art-exhibition/

are loved, accepted and have nothing to prove. And this knowledge will ensure that our hearts remain open, connected and creative. Unlike the people of Israel we will reject violence, and we will still be able to sing, in whatever foreign land we may find ourselves.

to do

Set aside some time in your day to be free, for a few moments, of the usual busyness and distractedness, and to focus on listening to and becoming aware of God. As you prepare yourself, offer a brief prayer of thanksgiving for God's love and presence in your life. Invite God to open your eyes, your ears and your heart so that you can connect deeply with the Spirit. Now deepen your breathing, close your eyes and open your hands. Don't try to force anything, but allow a sense of being enfolded in God's presence to arise in you. Allow your imagination to expand to include the room where you are sitting, the neighborhood around you, the city, the nation and even the world. When you are ready, end with a prayer of thanksgiving, and a request that God's presence remain with you through the day. Then seek to remain intentionally aware as you go through your daily tasks.

to pray

Remind me, O God, that when I live in you I am always at home.

day twenty~one

a life of invocation

His father said to him, "Look, dear son, you have always stayed by me, and everything I have is yours." – Luke 15:31

Until our thoughts of God have found every visible thing and event glorious with his presence, the word of Jesus has not yet fully seized us. – Dallas Willard

to read
Luke 15:11-32

to think about
"We were political opponents, but around my daughter's hospital bed, we were brothers and sisters in Christ." I watched his eyes fill with tears as this past mayor of our little town recalled one of the most tragic and healing moments of his life. In the dying years of apartheid, he had been a member of the Conservative Party and had worked hard to keep apartheid alive. But now he was forced to negotiate with representatives of the recently unbanned African National Congress, whom he viewed as godless Communists.

Then a car accident left his daughter in a coma. Her chances of survival were slim, and doctors warned that, even if she did recover, she would probably be severely incapacitated. Daily he and his wife prayed by her bedside, asking that God would heal her and restore her to them.

One day, when he got to her hospital room, he found a group of black men and women gathered around her. He immediately recognized them as negotiators from the ANC. As he entered the ward, they asked if he would allow them to pray for his daughter. They stood together, with eyes closed and hearts joined in intercession, and the world of this large white South African father changed completely. Where before the lines had been clear, they were now blurred. The people praying for his daughter had been a religious and ideological threat, but now he found them to be allies in faith. God, it suddenly seemed to him, could not be so easily contained. In the following months, he finished his term as mayor, he changed his political affiliation, his daughter returned to almost complete health, and he discovered that his family in Christ was far bigger than he had ever imagined.

In an attempt to explain to his followers the wideness of God's mercy and grace, Jesus told the story of a gracious father whose son was determined to experience the world. After asking for his share of the inheritance, the boy went off to squander his wealth on wild and narcissistic living. His elder brother remained at home, faithfully continuing to work alongside his father. After some time, the younger son returned in shame when the money ran out. His delighted and forgiving father threw a party for him, but the elder brother was angry.

"All these years I've slaved for you and never once refused to do a single thing you told me to", he complained. "And in all that time you never gave me even one young goat for a feast with my friends." The response Jesus put in the father's mouth was a call for his hearers to change both how they saw the world, and how they lived in it. "Look, dear son, you have always stayed by me, and everything I have is yours..."

In his quest to be good and obedient, this son had failed to understand the generosity of his father. The abundance that was all around was available to him at all times, but either he had not realized this, or he had failed to believe it. It was not only his younger brother who had squandered their father's gifts. Both of them were wasteful of his grace, love, and generosity. If they had only been able to recognize and receive their father's goodness, they would both have discovered a life of joy, fullness and connection.

When our God is too small – like the man who did not believe his political opponents could share his faith – we live small lives. When, like the brother of the prodigal son, we make our lives about legalistic duty, we miss out on the amazing joy and celebration that God offers us. It is all too easy to hide God away in a church building, or to hoard God's grace, keeping it only for those whom we believe are truly "worthy". People of faith have made this mistake for centuries, with destructive results.

The practice of invocation shows us another way. It is not just a prayer, but a way of living. It teaches us constantly to be aware of God's presence and activity in our world. It trains us to remain open to the constant work of God's Spirit in our hearts. And it changes how we experience and engage every moment and every interaction of our lives.

As followers of Christ, we are called to make our lives a constant invocation. Jesus has revealed to us that our world is flooded with God's presence, that spirit and matter are inseparably united, and that even our own bodies are dwelling places of the Spirit. In response, we need only stay attuned to God's presence, and to live from this new, wider, deeper and more complete understanding of the world.

When we live a life of constant invocation, always inviting God to make God's self known to us and through us, we become the most "at home" people in the world. We know that we are accepted and loved by God, because we constantly sense God's nearness. We know that we are unique and precious because we experience God's Spirit within every part of our being. We know that others are equally loved because we are learning to see God's presence in them – even if they aren't aware of it themselves. We know that our whole cosmos is alive and shining with the glory of God, because we have learned to recognize the signs.

This "invocationary" way of being impacts how we pray, how we care for ourselves, how we treat others, and how we live on this planet. It inspires us to work to grow in our awareness of God, and to help others to see in us what we are learning to see in everything. And when we have come to know, in the deepest part of ourselves, that this really is "our Father's world",[1] nothing can take from us the wonderful, life-giving sense of belonging that is ours.

to do

Start your day by allowing yourself to become aware again of God's presence within and around you. Take a moment to give thanks and celebrate your belonging in God's love and in God's world. Now go into the day intent on extending God's welcome to every person and every creature you encounter. Although it may feel strange, you may want to borrow St. Francis' habit of referring to different parts of creation as brother or sister, in order to remind yourself of how everything is connected in God's love and presence.[2]

to pray

As you always welcome me within your presence, O God, so today I welcome the universe into my heart.

---

[1] This idea comes from a hymn written by Maltbie D. Babcock and Franklin L. Sheppard. The lyrics can be found here: http://www.hymnsite.com/lyrics/umh144.sht (accessed 27 September 2012)

[2] To get an idea of what this might mean, see the Wikipedia article about the Canticle of the Sun: http://en.wikipedia.org/wiki/Canticle_of_the_Sun (accessed 27 September 2012)

to explore together

ICE BREAKER

Have you ever had a deep experience of God's presence, or God's Spirit? What was it like, and what impact did it have on you?

WORSHIP

Begin by sharing your thoughts and experiences of God's Spirit. Then, sing or read a hymn or poem that invites God's presence to be with you.

Move into a time of gentle preparation. Deepen your breathing and open your hands. Imagine that you are placing into them anything that keeps you from connecting with God. When you are ready, turn your hands palms down and imagine that you are handing all of these distractions over to God. Then, turn your palms up again, and open yourself to receive a new sense of being filled by God's Spirit. Sit in silence in this attitude of receiving for as long as you desire.

Close with a prayer or song of thanksgiving.

READING

Romans 8:14-26

DISCUSSION QUESTIONS

1. What stood out for you in this week's reflections?
2. To what extent have you viewed the world as divided, with spirit and matter separate? How has this affected your life?
3. What does it mean to be God's children filled with God's Spirit according to Romans 8? How have you experienced this?
4. How can you practice invocation in your own life?
5. How does living with a sense of God's presence help you feel at home in the world?

week four

GREETING

In this new life, it doesn't matter if you are a Jew or a Gentile, circumcised or uncircumcised, barbaric, uncivilized, slave, or free. Christ is all that matters, and He lives in all of us.
– Colossians 3:11

Remember that community is a state of being together in which people, instead of hiding behind their defenses, learn to lower them, in which instead of attempting to obliterate their differences, people learn not only to accept them but rejoice in them.
– M. Scott Peck

thought for the week:

After just two years, the Civility Project was disbanded. It was launched by Mark DeMoss, a conservative evangelical Christian, and a Republican, on the eve of Barack Obama's inauguration. He was joined by Lanny Davis, a liberal Jewish Democrat. Together they asked people across the country to sign a simple pledge committing to civility in public discourse, and to stand against incivility. Although many ordinary citizens signed the pledge, only three members of the United States Congress were willing to do so.[1]

It is easy to fall into comfortable lives in which we acknowledge only those who think, act and look the same as we do. It is easy to become dismissive of those who are different. But, such carelessness does not create a peaceful and healthy world. It fosters resentments, division and hatred, often leading to violence and destruction.

Yet, we all long to feel safe, welcomed, and at home in the world. To reach this dream may be far less complicated than we imagine. It may well be as simple as choosing to embrace civility. It may be as easy as just greeting our neighbors and being welcoming toward those who are different from us. And even if these small gestures are insufficient to make any significant difference, they certainly can't hurt.

When we gather for worship we are usually invited to greet one another. This is not just about murmuring a quick "hello" to a few people around us. It's about learning to be people of welcome, people who are open to others. If we want to be at home in the world, to feel like we belong, this habit of greeting is one that we really need to learn.

---

[1] For more information see the Civility Project website at www.CivilityProject.org or this article in the Huffington Post: http://www.huffingtonpost.com/2011/01/12/mark-demoss-civility-project_n_808219.html (both accessed 13 October 2012)

day twenty-two

the downside of uniformity

The man wanted to justify his actions, so he asked Jesus, "And who is my neighbor?" – Luke 10:29

You don't get harmony when everybody sings the same note.
– Doug Floyd

to read

Luke 10:25-37

to think about

When the group gave wrong answers, seventy-five percent of people followed at least once. This was the finding in a series of studies performed by psychologist Solomon Asch in the 1950s. Asch invited students at Swarthmore College to participate in what he called a vision test. The truth was that only one of the students in each group was being tested, while the others (usually numbering between five and seven) were collaborating with the experiment. The groups were shown pairs of cards. On the first card in every pair was a single line. On the second card three lines of different lengths appeared. The group was asked to match the length of one of the three lines on the second card with the line on the first. In the first two pairs, the collaborators gave the correct answer, but after that they deliberately gave wrong answers about two-thirds of the time.

Imagine being the only person in the room who sees something different from everyone else. How would you respond as you heard the others giving answers that you alone were convinced were wrong? The pressure to conform in Asch's experiments was revealed to be very strong, and the proportion of people who went along with the group, *even when they knew the group was wrong*, was significantly high. However, when even one additional person disagreed with the group, subjects immediately expressed their true opinions, and the proportion of people who followed the group plummeted.[1]

This pressure to conform, which often results in groups of people becoming less intelligent than the individuals in the group, is what psychologist Irving Janis called "Groupthink". While we may celebrate that "birds of a feather flock together", when they do, it impacts the group negatively in all sorts of ways. This desire for uniformity and conformity is one of the great dangers of religion. Over the centuries, churches have often adopted marketing and community-building strategies that separate people according to how alike they are. We place children in one room, youth in another and seniors in a third. We have groups for women, for men, for singles and for marrieds. We have gatherings for pretty much every conceivable preference in musical style, liturgical format and theological opinion. But, the more we insist on gathering only with those who are like us, the less we all become like Christ, and the less effective we become in fulfilling God's mission.

When a religious leader asked Jesus how eternal life could be gained, Jesus responded with what we now know as the Great Commandment. It seems that the man was uncomfortable with the implications of Jesus' answer, though, and so he asked Jesus to define who his "neighbor" was. In response Jesus told the story of the Good Samaritan. This parable was

---

[1] For more information about Asch's conformity experiments, see this Wikipedia article: http://en.wikipedia.org/wiki/Asch_conformity_experiments (accessed 28 September 2012)

both a call to compassion and a call to diversity, and it revealed how the two go hand in hand.

The man who was beaten and left for dead in this story was Jewish, but when his Jewish religious leaders passed by, they all ignored him. In a world where we believe that only those who are like us are loved by God and worthy of friendship, our hearts grow small. When we see someone who is different from us – even if only in circumstance – our tendency is to withdraw and retreat back into our neat, uniform worlds. This is how Jesus described the priest and the Temple assistant in his parable.

The person who did finally help the wounded man could hardly have been more different from him. As a Samaritan, he would have been hated and rejected by any faithful Jewish person, and he would have been expected to respond in kind. But, the man in Jesus' story is clearly far more comfortable with diversity. His heart is open not only to his own people, but to anyone in need, and so he goes out of his way to help and heal. This is how Jesus calls his followers to live.

Such open-heartedness is not nurtured in sanitized, uniform communities. We don't learn to love when the only ones we will accept are those who reflect ourselves back to us. We don't learn to live when the only world we engage is the one that can fit into our preconceptions. We don't become creative by remaining within the same, uniform environment. We don't discover anything new when we demonize what is different. We don't experience the breadth and depth of God's nature by seeing God's image only in our own faces. Uniformity and conformity may have their place in human affairs, but not in the community of faith.

For most of us this is a massive struggle. It does not come naturally for us to move out of our culture and our comfort zones. It is far easier to limit our connections to those with whom we agree, and from whom we can expect little challenge, surprise or conflict. It takes the willingness to choose and the effort to do the work, for us to reach out to those who are unlike us. But the alternative is to doom ourselves to a bland life of uniformity and conformity.

It is troubling that the Christian faith is often perceived as "secluded" and disconnected from the diversity of God's extravagantly creative world. As Jonathan, a twenty-two-year-old American, put it: "Christians enjoy being in their own community. The more they seclude themselves, the less they can function in the real world. So many Christians are caught in the Christian "bubble".[2] These words apply not just to the relationship Christians have with the world outside of their churches, but to the scandalous tendency we have to gather in uniform groups within our churches. It may feel good to connect with those who affirm our points of view, and who share our culture, but what feels good is not always what leads us to life.

to do

Think about the people with whom you most often spend time. How similar are they to you? How many friends or close associates do you have that are significantly different from you in race, religion, philosophy, gender, sexual orientation or age? In what ways have you idolized uniformity and conformity in your own life, and in what ways are you connecting with the diversity and creativity of the world? Respond to these reflections by offering a prayer of confession, if necessary, and then go into your day with a commitment to connect with those who are different from you.

to pray

Forgive me, O God, when I protect myself from difference.

---

[2] Quoted in David Kinnaman and Gabe Lyons, *UnChristian: What a New Generation Really Thinks About Christianity...And Why It Matters*, (Grand Rapids, Baker Books, 2007), 121.

the gift of diversity

Then He appointed twelve of them and called them
His apostles. – Mark 3:14

We're all only fragile threads, but what a tapestry we make.
– Jerry Ellis

to read

Mark 3:13-19

to think about

Her father lost his job. She was threatened with poison, and a white woman protested by placing a black baby doll inside a wooden coffin. She was six years old, and all she had done to earn these repercussions was to go to school.

In 1960, Ruby Bridges was one of six black children chosen to attend "white" schools in Louisiana after the court ordered that they should be desegregated. But, on November 14, as Ruby braved the protesting crowds outside William Frantz Elementary School, she was alone apart from her parents. Three of the selected children attended a different school together, and two had decided to remain in the safety of their old schools.

As a result of the angry protests by white parents, Ruby's first day was spent in the principal's office, and for a year, the local teachers refused to teach her. Instead Ruby sat in a classroom alone, with a teacher who had been brought in from Boston, Massachusetts. It was a painful and frightening time for her and the other black children, but without their courage, and that of their parents, American society would have remained divided. It is not surprising that over fifty years later, Ruby, whose last name is now Hall, tours as an inspirational speaker against racism.[1]

The hatred and division that marked American society in the 1960s is not uncommon in human experience. In South Africa we know the destructive consequences of discrimination first hand, and in first century Palestine it was no different. That's why, when Jesus proclaimed that God's Reign was "at hand", he established an intentionally diverse community to show what it looked like. It's easy to read the list of the apostles' names and miss the miracle that Jesus was bringing into being.

Among his twelve chosen were James and John, two brothers with such a bad case of sibling rivalry that they were known as "Sons of Thunder". Along with Peter and Andrew they were fisherman – ordinary Jewish entrepreneurs who would have hated Matthew, the tax collector to whom they, or others like them, would have paid exorbitant taxes. And, in any other circumstances, Matthew would have feared for his life if he had encountered Simon, the zealot – a freedom fighter who was committed to the overthrow of the Roman Empire and its collaborators. Simon would probably also have been a threat to Philip, whose Greek name, and link to the Greek community,[2] suggest that his family may have been Hellenists – Jews who had integrated the culture of the pagan Greeks into their Hebrew faith – a practice which, for some, made them "impure". Jesus deliberately called together a group of people who were most unlikely to get along and then,

---

[1] For more information about Ruby Bridges Hall and the integration of American schools, see this Wikipedia article: http://en.wikipedia.org/wiki/Ruby_Bridges (accessed 2 October 2012)

[2] See John 12:20-36.

in order to demonstrate what God's Reign was like, instructed them to live together and love one another.

Jesus' choice of apostles reveals two profound truths that the Rabbi was seeking to proclaim. The first is that God's Reign is open to all. The moment we try to close the doors of God's welcome to anyone, we cease to reflect the radical inclusivity of Jesus' message and mission. The second truth that Jesus knew is that diversity is a gift that we desperately need to learn to embrace. These apostles were all so very different in temperament and abilities, but when the time came for the Church to be established and the Gospel to be proclaimed to the world, it was this diversity that made the new Christian community so effective.

It's tempting to believe that diversity should occur "naturally". We justify our tendency to gravitate to those who are like us by saying that we don't want to "force" an "unnatural" togetherness. The Gospel does not allow us this refuge. What Jesus taught, in word and action, was the same thing that the black people of Louisiana knew. People of different races, backgrounds and cultures only come together when they choose to. It takes an intentional commitment for us to overcome our fear of one another's differences and find a connection. But, when we are willing to do the work, the gifts that we receive from being part of a diverse community are priceless.

When we open ourselves to those who are different from us we enter a world of creativity and learning that is hidden when we remain only with those who are like us. When we spend time with "strangers", we experience new things in our world, but also in ourselves. We learn new truths and new ways of doing things that enrich and expand our lives. We discover new experiences and ways of seeing God and God's world.

Daniel Goleman, author of *Social Intelligence*, surmises that the benefits of learning compassion for one another could range "from higher achievement in school to better performance at work, from happier and more socially able children to better community safety and lifetime health".[3]

Learning to love one another, as hard as it may be, is not just a religious duty, but a necessary skill for the health and survival of our world. But we don't learn to cross the boundaries of our differences unless we deliberately choose to. This is why, as followers of Christ, we are called into community where we can spend a lifetime learning to love, and discovering the gifts that connection brings.

to do

Think about all the different people that fill your world – family members, friends, co-workers, employees, passers-by. Allow their faces to rise up in your memory and spend a moment honoring them for who they are. Some you know really well, and some you may not know at all, but each is unique, and each is very different from you. Take a moment to acknowledge the special gifts that each one brings into your life, and then offer a prayer of praise for God's diverse creation and of thanks for all the people who enrich your life.

to pray

For all the different people who fill my world, O God, I give you thanks and praise.

---

[3] Goleman, Daniel, *Social Intelligence – The New Science of Human Relationships,* (London, Hutchinson, 2006), 317.

day twenty~four

a diverse community

But as the believers rapidly multiplied, there were rumblings of discontent. – Acts 6:1a

The great enemy of community is exclusivity. Groups that exclude others because they are poor or doubters or divorced or sinners or of some different race or nationality are not communities; they are cliques – actually defensive bastions against community. – M. Scott Peck

to read

Acts 6:1-7

to think about

"They don't want us there on Sunday. It makes too many people nervous." The boy who spoke these words looked scary enough that some concerned citizen had called the police. He had dyed-black hair shaped into long spikes, tattoos on both arms and one leg, and piercings through his ears, nose, lips and eyebrows. Both he, and the friend who was with him, wore baggy clothes and had been riding skateboards in the church parking lot. It was the presence of the rather aggressive policeman that drew the pastor of the church out to investigate. He noticed that both boys were responding politely, in spite of how they were being harassed, and so he reassured the policeman that they were doing nothing wrong. The two boys thanked him and then mentioned that they had to get going to the Episcopal church where they were working in the soup kitchen. Three days of every week they served soup to the homeless, and every Friday they each tutored a special needs child. But, in spite of this, they felt no welcome from the community in which they served. So, on Sunday they were nowhere to be seen.[1]

To live in community is very difficult, which is why many of us refuse to even attempt it. When we are challenged to embrace diversity within our communities, we become even less interested in the quest. In response many of us are tempted to live out our faith only in groups of like-minded believers, making sure that those who look or think differently from us know that they are not welcome. Or we abandon the call to community altogether, and try to follow Jesus alone. But, the moment we do this, we cease to really be the people of God.

As James Smith points out, the biblical vision of God's Reign is of a community called from "every tribe and language and people and nation".[2] But, the scandal of our faith is that our churches don't resemble this diversity in any significant way. As we gather, we may notice that most of our companions look a lot like us. We may also notice other Christians, who are different from us but similar to one another, gathering in other churches.[3] This tragic reality may be comfortable, but it robs us of the life, joy and growth that God's Reign offers, and it undermines our witness to the world.

This struggle to come together in God's name is not new.

---

[1] This story comes from a much larger blog post about young people and the church. It is worth reading the entire piece (including the comments): http://doroteos2.wordpress.com/2012/06/28/beyond-label-or-category/ (accessed 9 October 2012)

[2] Revelation 5:9

[3] See Smith, James, K.A., *Desiring the Kingdom – Worship, Worldview and Cultural Formation*, (Grand Rapids, Baker Academic, 2009), 161-162.

From the first days of the Church, people wrestled with what it meant to be a diverse Christian community. Where the various religions of the time comfortably allowed like-minded people to create their own, unique sub-cultures, Christianity called people from every background to share life together. This meant that Jews, who were circumcised and followed the laws of food and hygiene, found themselves living with Gentiles who knew nothing of the law. Inevitably conflicts arose, as the various factions and groups tried to cling to "their" ways, while embracing the new way of Jesus. Even as the church served those who were marginalized – feeding widows, orphans and beggars – some people complained about favoritism and unfairness. This became such a massive issue that the apostles had to appoint special deacons to deal with the problem. But even then, the struggle with diversity remained. Throughout his ministry Paul constantly challenged the churches under his care to give up their factions and sub-cultures and come together as a new people in Christ. Yet, centuries later, we still haven't learned to be the loving, diverse community that Jesus calls us to be.

In spite of the church's failure to embody the vision of a diverse community, the call remains. God still challenges us to learn to love one another through the misunderstandings and uncertainties. We are still called to be less easily offended and more committed to understanding and making space for one another.

As the world wrestles to find ways to overcome the divisions of race, gender, culture, language, religion, sexuality and economic status, it needs models that can demonstrate what a diverse but unified community looks like. It is the glorious mission of the church to be such a model. It is our calling to lead the way to peace and justice by showing what it means to love one another, not just *in spite of* our differences, but *because of* them. When we can truly learn to celebrate and learn from what makes us each unique, we will begin to touch the miracle of God's Reign in our time and space.

To embody God's vision of community requires each of us to make some significant shifts in our thinking and behavior.

We have to learn that "different" does not equal "wrong". We have to learn to listen first and pronounce later (if at all). We have to release our need to be right in favor of our need to be in relationship. We have to leave judgements to God, and we have to give up trying to change one another. But, perhaps above all, we each need to commit to being people who choose to love and forgive, regardless of how others may treat us.

It is only when we are willing to stake our lives on the cross, to embrace suffering for the sake of the new world that Jesus died to establish, that we can begin to be the welcoming, inclusive, loving community of which God dreams. But, as difficult as it may be, the healing, joy and blessing that true community offers is worth every tear and every ounce of sweat. We may never fully achieve God's ideal community, but we can try each day to move a little closer to it.

to do

Spend some time in quiet prayer. Remember God's vision for the Church, and pray that it may become what God dreams. Pray for your own local church community, and ask God to enable you to help it to become a safe, diverse place of welcome. Now spend a few moments thinking of the people, both in the church and outside of it, with whom you most struggle to connect. Ask God to show you how to love, forgive and understand them. Open your heart to any insights or ideas that might lead you to be more welcoming and accepting, and commit to go through the day with an open and loving heart.

to pray

Teach me to welcome those who are different from me, Jesus, even as you have welcomed me.

day twenty~five

CReating community

Everyone listened quietly as Barnabas and Paul told about the miraculous signs and wonders God had done through them among the Gentiles. – Acts 15:12

He drew a circle that shut me out –
Heretic, rebel, a thing to flout.
But Love and I had the wit to win:
We drew a circle that took him in.
– Edwin Markham

to Read

Acts 15:1-12

to think about

"Somehow a miracle happened. No more pollution." This unexpected result was achieved by a very surprising, but very simple, act of kindness.

On a nice plot with a vegetable garden surrounded by lilacs, a family of eight shared their lives. Behind their property was a tenement block whose residents would casually throw their rubbish into the garden. The children were indignant, suggesting that the polluters should be reprimanded. But, their mother simply instructed them to go out and pick some of the lilacs, and then take a bouquet to each family in the tenement, saying that their mother had thought they might enjoy them. It was this small gift that brought an end to the pollution.[1]

The moment we seek to live in community, and the instant we accept that true community authentically reflects the diversity of its members, we face the tough task of learning to live with one another. Wherever two or three are gathered, differences will arise, and disputes will eventually occur. Whenever we come together with others, our griefs and wounds, our celebrations and joys, begin to emerge, and sometimes they clash with those of our companions. While we may try to build community in ways that seek to avoid conflict, these attempts will fail. Our quest for polite peace may feel like the road to true community, but in fact, what we end up with is "pseudocommunity" – a state in which we pretend to be open and committed to one another, but in which no one is really able to be authentic and honest.[2]

From the beginning the church wrestled with the difficult challenge of community, and had to learn the skills and open-heartedness that could bring groups of very different people into a cohesive whole. The new Christian community wrestled with the question of whether the law should be a requirement for both Jews and Gentiles, and the leaders had to find ways to resolve these differences creatively and with integrity. Although they never completely removed the judgements and grumblings of those who insisted on having their own way, their commitment to each other enabled them to build a church that changed the world forever.

The first believers didn't achieve true community through polite avoidance of conflict, or denial of the differences between them. Rather, they became a transforming community by honestly working through their struggles. The book of Acts shows the first believers taking time to meet, to

---

[1] This story was told to Leo Aikman of the *Atlanta Constitution*. It is related in Stephen R. Covey's book *Everyday Greatness,* (Nashville, Rutledge Hill Press, 2006), 345.

[2] For a discussion of pseudocommunity see M. Scott Peck, *The Different Drum,* (London, Rider & Co., reprint of 1989), 86-90.

debate, to pray, and to wrestle until they found a way forward together. Sometimes they confronted each other strongly and bluntly, but always, their commitment to one another and to the shared vision of God's Reign ensured that they put relationship above all.[3]

For this kind of community to happen, we need to be willing to participate in creating good "containers" for our life together. A container, as William Isaacs explains, is a setting in which the work of human connection can most effectively be done.[4] In much of our lives we simply react to one another, and we find that we are unable to "hold" the intensity of our emotions, experiences and grievances. But, when we have an effective container in which to interact, our ability to carry one another's views and emotions is enhanced.

A good container for community includes an effective space in which to interact, sufficient time to listen and communicate without feeling rushed or forced to compete to be heard, and an attitude of openness and solidarity toward one another. When we put these ingredients in place, we are far more likely to be able to resolve our struggles successfully, to feel safe enough to connect with one another authentically, and to carry the weight of one another's griefs and celebrations.

We are all participants in creating these containers. When we succeed, we learn to listen without judging – holding the ideas and emotions of the other person with humility and respect, even if they are expressed strongly. We learn to adopt a stance of inclusion, in which people are considered to belong unless or until *they* choose to opt out. And we learn to respond from an attitude of curiosity, seeking understanding, rather than a position of "giving advice" or trying to "fix" the other person. When we find ourselves in relationships with others where we know that we are welcomed and accepted as we are, even if we disagree with one another, we are all deeply healed and we find a sense of true belonging.

---

[3] See, for example, Paul's strong confrontation of Peter in Galatians 2:11-16.

[4] See Isaacs, William, *Dialogue and the Art of Thinking Together*, (New York, Currency, 1999), 239-251.

The church provides a number of different containers in which to do this work. The weekly worship gathering is one in which we are able to celebrate our life together, recognize our diversity, and discover what it means to be part of something bigger than "our" group of friends and family. Most churches also have a variety of different kinds of small groups and ministries in which people can share their lives more deeply and authentically.

The key to making all of these community-building opportunities work is to keep God's vision of true community in our hearts, to commit to a group that enables us to connect deeply with others, and to choose an attitude of openness, listening and, when necessary, forgiveness toward our companions in faith.

to do

Spend a moment in quiet reflection and try to connect with your own need to belong. Remember that other people share this same longing, and pray for them, even as you pray for yourself. Now thank God that as you give yourself to create a safe place of belonging for others, you find one for yourself. Spend today taking every opportunity to create such safe spaces for everyone you meet.

to pray

As I give myself to connect with others in your name, Jesus, so I find a place in your community for myself.

day twenty~six

the powerful act of greeting

Then Barnabas brought him to the apostles and told them how Saul had seen the Lord on the way to Damascus... – Acts 9:27a

Heroes were ordinary people who knew that even if their own lives were impossibly knotted, they could untangle someone else's. And maybe that one act could lead someone to rescue you right back. – Jodi Picoult

to read
Acts 9:26-28

to think about

I was determined that I was not going to make eye contact. This is a survival strategy that is adopted by many South Africans as we are confronted by vendors of various kinds at almost every traffic light in every major city. If you look at them, we think, they've got you, and you'll end up spending money you don't have on something you don't need.

But, this time, my strategy didn't work. I was one of only a few cars waiting for the light to change as a man holding a bottle of water and a cloth ran over and offered to wash my windscreen. Keeping my eyes averted I shook my head and hoped he would move on. But then I noticed his brown face leaning across my windscreen. I tried to look away, but he just kept leaning until his face was right in front of mine. Then, when I could avoid his eyes no more, he smiled and waved. I had no choice but to smile and wave in return. In that moment I realized that all he wanted was to be *seen* – to be acknowledged as a fellow human being, and to be treated with respect and dignity. As I drove away, I felt ashamed at my defensiveness, and I resolved to work harder to see those around me more carefully, and to greet them with respect.

The Zulu greeting *siyabona* means "I see you". In his motion picture, *Avatar*, James Cameron used these words to great effect, revealing, in the different ways the characters greeted one another, the power of really seeing another person.[1] If we are to find a place to belong, if we are to learn to live well in community, we need to learn the gift of seeing and the power in a simple, respectful greeting.

After his dramatic conversion experience, the apostle Paul returned to Jerusalem. The believers there were afraid of him, though, because the last they had heard was that he was persecuting the church. But, where others kept their distance out of fear and suspicion, Barnabas reached out to this new disciple. He befriended Paul (who was still known as Saul at this time) and brought him to the leaders of the community. He introduced the new convert and explained his story, inviting them to see him in a new light. It was this act of seeing, welcoming and greeting that gave Paul a place in the church and made it possible for him to become such an effective apostle. When we think about the letters that Paul wrote in all his years of ministry, we can be grateful to Barnabas. It is because of his openness to Paul that a large proportion of our New Testament came into being.

Every Sunday, in churches across the world, God-seekers gather in the name of Christ. We hear the call to worship, and we invoke God's Spirit to connect us with God and help us to live out our faith in the coming week. Then, in an act that is often treated with little thought, we greet one another. We

---

[1] Cameron, James (Director), 2009, *Avatar*, United States, Twentieth Century Fox.

may use formal words (here or later in the service) such as "The peace of the Lord be with you", or we may just say hello. There may be some laughter as we chat with friends, or awkwardness as we acknowledge strangers. There may even be a few introverts (like me) who pretend to be busy with something else in order to avoid being touched by others. But, in this one disorganized moment, we are doing something that is deeply meaningful, and very important for the community we are trying to build. We are choosing to deliberately *see* one another.

We cannot hope to build strong and deep connections with people who are different from us if we insist on keeping them at arm's length. We cannot find friendship and belonging if we keep our distance until others make the first move. The act of greeting offers us a safe way to take the initiative and "cross the room" to make a connection with one another.

Of course, the basis for our greeting of one another is God's all-embracing greeting of us. It is God who has welcomed us into God's family. It is God who, in Christ, has taken the initiative and "crossed the room" to connect with us. As we gather for worship, we recognize that we are, in a sense, guests in God's house who are seen by God, greeted by God and welcomed by God. But then, as we find our place in God's household, we become hosts who must learn to see one another, greet one another and welcome each other in God's name. As God's greeting of us has been open, inclusive, gracious and forgiving, so we strive to greet one another with the same inclusive grace. It is a moment of laying aside our differences and our disagreements and affirming that, despite all that might divide us, we are one in Christ.

The act of greeting in worship is not just a quick "hello" to break the ice and make us feel a little more comfortable with the "others" who have gathered for worship. It is an act that proclaims – to us and to the world – that we belong in God's household, and that we willingly make space for others to belong as well. It is a moment in which we envision what the world would be like if we could learn to move beyond our stereotypes and assumptions, our grievances and non-negotiables, and really *see* one another. It is an act of affirming our common humanity, our shared desire for God, and our dependence on God and one another for life.

In the moment of greeting, what matters is not that our lives are "tangled", but that we are committed to helping "untangle" each other, and that we allow ourselves to be channels of God's healing love and grace to one another. When we gather for worship and greet each other, we are making the difficult and transforming choice to honor each other, to practice kindness toward each other, and to embrace the risk of connecting.

to do

Today take a moment to think about the people that are closest to you – your family and friends. Then expand your thinking to include others with whom you regularly interact – coworkers or worshippers at your church, perhaps. Now, begin to think about the people whom you regularly interact with, but have not really seen. Cleaners or checkout people at the grocery store. Take a moment to celebrate the humanity of each person. As you go through the day, greet everyone as a way of helping you to really see them.

to pray

As you have seen and welcomed me, O God, so I choose to see and welcome others.

day twenty~seven

WITNESSES

Then He turned to the woman and said to Simon, "Look at this woman kneeling here…" – Luke 7:44a

The main concern of Wholehearted men and women is living a life defined by courage, compassion, and connection.
– Brené Brown

to read

Luke 7:36-50

to think about

"If you open your heart, just a crack, to God, God will come rushing in." I heard these words repeated almost every week for months. I was part of a team of Christian students who conducted weekly worship services at a seniors' home in a poor township in Grahamstown, South Africa. Each week, after the formal liturgy, we would spend time sharing tea and chatting with the elderly residents, and each week I would find myself sitting on the floor at the feet of an old man who shared my first name.

Smiling through the few teeth he had left and gesturing with tobacco-stained fingers, John would talk about his children, whom he hadn't seen for years. He would confess to his past addiction to alcohol, and to the many mistakes he had made in his life. And then, with eyes becoming moist and shiny, he would express his gratitude for the grace that God had shown him, and the salvation he had found. He always ended our chat reminding me to open my heart to God, so that God could come rushing in. To this day, whenever I feel my heart growing cold and closed, John's words challenge me to stay open.

It was uncommon in the early eighties for young white students to spend time with elderly colored folk, and they often expressed their gratitude. But I remain convinced that the greatest gift was not given by us, but by these old, forgotten men and women to us. They taught us what it meant to really see and connect with one another.

It was pretty common to find Jesus enjoying the hospitality of his followers. At times he was even criticized for his choice of mealtime companions.[1] But, he was not exclusive. He accepted invitations from society's outcasts and from the elite, which is how he came to be at the home of a Pharisee named Simon. It is not clear why Simon invited Jesus, but the meal certainly did not proceed as he had expected. They were interrupted by a woman of dubious reputation, who knelt behind Jesus weeping as she washed his feet with her tears, wiped them dry with her hair, kissed them and poured perfume over them. The Pharisee was shocked and offended, although he tried to hide it. All his stereotypes played through his mind as he questioned Jesus' discernment for allowing such a show from such a woman.

But, then Jesus draws Simon into the spectacle with a parable about the love that flows from cancelled debts. Simon cannot do anything but agree that the person who is forgiven the most will love the most. In response, Jesus instructs him to do a simple, but deeply significant thing: "Look at this woman kneeling here." Until that moment, the Pharisee had not really seen her. She was nothing more than her past, her immoral profession, and her embarrassing display of emotion. Any humanity, any personhood that she had, had been erased in Simon's mind. As the conversation continues, it becomes clear that the same was true of Simon's treatment of Jesus. All the usual courtesy for a guest had been ignored, and

---

[1] Matthew 9:11

Jesus had been reduced to his strange ideas, and his undesirable associations.

Jesus enjoyed living in community, seeing the richness and worth of each person, and drawing them to connect with their true selves, with one another and with God. Simon, on the other hand, had no understanding or experience of true community. Simon's life was well regulated, shaped by law and ritual, and by the requirements of his social status. This all made it very hard for him to really see another person – especially one who fell outside of his standards of morality or civility. And when you cannot see someone, you cannot form any kind of relationship.

Every human being knows the longing to be truly seen. We all yearn for a connection with another person that is strong and safe enough for us to reveal the truth about ourselves and to be known, accepted, and loved. In the movie, *Shall We Dance?* Beverley Clark (played by Susan Sarandon) hires Devine, a private investigator, because she suspects that her husband is having an affair. When she receives the news that the "affair" is actually a dancing class, she finds herself opening up to Devine. In response to his question about why people get married she replies:

> Because we need a witness to our lives. There's a billion people on the planet, I mean, what does any one life really mean? But, in a marriage, you're promising to care about everything – the good things, the bad things, the terrible things, the mundane things – all of it, all the time, every day. You're saying, "Your life will not go unnoticed, because I will notice it. Your life will not go unwitnessed, because I will be your witness."[2]

But, it is not enough to have only one witness to our lives, and it is not enough to witness only one other life. Partners die and marriages fail, and it is impossible for one person to see everything. But, when we expand our network, we are seen by many others, and they each reflect something different back to us about ourselves. When we take the time

[2] Chelsom, Peter (Director), 2004, *Shall We Dance?* United States, Miramax.

to notice many others, our experience of the world expands and deepens.

Living in community means that our whole life – not just what we do on Sunday – is witnessed by our companions. It means that we have a ready crowd of cheerleaders to encourage us, and a trusted safety net to catch us when we fall. It means that our contributions to the world can be multiplied, and we can be held accountable for using our gifts. It means that we can be stretched and empowered, and that when we get to the end of our time on this planet, we will know that we have made a mark for the better. But, living in community also means that we become all of these things to others, some of whom may never be noticed in any other way. And it means that, as we recognize and celebrate the humanity of every person – even those we might consider the "least" – our own humanity is affirmed and healed.

to ∂o

Think about the situations and people in the world that you usually prefer not to think about. Reflect, for a moment, on how choices like these – to avoid witnessing the lives and suffering of others – diminishes these other people. Now consider the way in which God has noticed your life (Read Psalm 8 if you need to get a sense of this), and has given you friends and family to be your witnesses. Now offer a prayer of thanks, and go into the day resolved to be a witness to others – especially the "least".

to pRay

Thank you, God, for noticing my life, and for calling me to be a witness to others.

day twenty~eight
the greeting life

And Jesus replied, "I assure you, today you will be with Me in paradise." – Luke 23:43

We are not held back by the love we didn't receive in the past, but by the love we're not extending in the present.
– Marianne Williamson

to read
Luke 23:32-43

to think about

"What if I just kept wearing my nametag?"

As a twenty-year-old student, Scott Ginsberg attended a seminar at his university where the delegates were all given nametags. When the seminar was over, he noticed that people immediately removed the tags and threw them away. But he was struck by the possibilities that might arise if he just kept wearing his nametag all the time.

What he discovered amazed him. Everywhere he went, people greeted him, and unexpected conversations began. He discovered that, while friendliness costs nothing, it brings immense value to human interactions. That was when he made the decision to keep wearing the nametag – every day for the rest of his life. That was a decade ago, and today he is known as the "Nametag Guy" – an international speaker and writer on approachability.

There are people who are offended by his friendliness. More than once he has had the tag ripped off his jacket by angry strangers. But, when this happens, he simply opens his jacket to reveal another nametag on his shirt, or he pulls a new, pre-written nametag out of his wallet and replaces the one that was removed. And, if that is not enough, he also has a nametag tattooed on his chest, proving his commitment to friendliness and approachability even in the face of hostility.[1]

I have no idea where Scott Ginsberg stands on the question of faith, but I believe that, in a world where religious people exclude, condemn and wage war on each other with tragic regularity, we could learn much from this man's simple commitment to make the world a friendlier place.

Jesus, of course, was even more committed to befriending and welcoming others – especially those who were considered unworthy of such notice. In the last few minutes of his life, as the nails of his executioners pierced his flesh, Jesus had every reason to close his heart and shut himself away in a prison of anger and bitterness. But, instead, he offered forgiveness to those who mocked and accused him. When one of the criminals dying beside him asked Jesus to notice and remember him, Jesus responded with kindness and compassion.

Remaining open to others did not free Jesus from the cross, but it did ensure that he died with the same integrity with which he had lived. And, throughout the centuries, it has continued to challenge his followers to adopt the same gracious, welcoming attitude. It is not overstating the case to say that the world is dying for us to live with this same open-hearted love.

It is a strange contradiction that we live in a world where we seem to be increasingly connected with one another, and yet, simultaneously, more isolated from each other. Social networks enable us to know intimate details of one another's lives, but the increasing insecurity of living in a time of

---

[1] For more information about Scott Ginsberg and his work on approachability, see his web site: www.hellomynameisscott.com (accessed 13 October 2012)

economic turmoil, political conflict and religious extremism often leads us to move into protected enclaves, separated from those who are different from us, and suspicious of strangers. In such a world, even the simple act of greeting a stranger can be viewed as suspicious or threatening.

But, for our world to become healthy, for our lives to become safer and more peaceful, we need more connection, not less. We need to learn the art of turning strangers, and even enemies, into friends. This means that we have to let go of our self-protection, and become more open to one another. We need to choose, consciously and consistently, to connect with those around us. In order to live in a civil, friendly world, we have to commit to civility and friendliness, by becoming approachable and welcoming.

This does not mean that we all have to wear nametags all the time. But it does mean that we have to learn to smile more easily, and greet one another more graciously. Being welcoming is not always comfortable. We will make mistakes. We will forget other people's names. We will make cultural blunders, and we will sometimes be rebuffed. But, comfort doesn't teach us anything new, and it doesn't help us grow into wholeness. It is when we are willing to reach across our differences, embrace the discomfort of new experiences and cultures, and open our hearts to those who challenge and question us, that we enter life's depths and breadths. It is when we choose to withhold judgement and put ourselves in the shoes of the other that we experience more of life's rich variety and wonder. And all it takes to enjoy all of these opportunities is a simple commitment to notice those around us and really greet them.

A greeting can be mere words that we speak politely out of convention. Or it can be the start of a connection. It can be an opening of the heart, and an invitation into a new relationship. It can be a way of engaging the world from a place of belonging, and a way of assuring those around us that they, too, belong. That's why Jesus taught his followers that "anyone who welcomes a little child like this on My behalf welcomes Me, and anyone who welcomes Me welcomes not only Me but also My Father who sent Me".[2]

It costs us nothing to say hello. But, when we make those words a code to live by, we gain a home and a family. We discover that, as different as we are from one another, in the most fundamental and important ways, we are the same. And we find that, through our simple friendliness, we help to make the world a place that reflects the gracious, loving friendship of Christ.

to do

Reflect, for a moment, on the kinds of situations in which you find it hard to greet strangers. Think about what holds you back, and ask yourself what you gain by your reticence. Then, try to imagine what you might be missing by not connecting with other people. Now, imagine what it would feel like to live in a world where everyone greeted and welcomed each other warmly. Make a commitment to help build that world by living a life of constant greeting.

to pray

Thank you, O God, that you always make the first move to connect with me, and that you enable me to do the same for others.

---

[2] Mark 9:37

to explore together

ICE BREAKER

What makes you unique, and how do you feel about it?

WORSHIP

Share together in a prayer of praise in which each person speaks out the names of as many different creatures, plants and natural objects as you can. Then, sing or read a hymn about creation.

In silence reflect on times when you have been tempted to view difference as wrong or bad. Ask for God's forgiveness, and invite God's Spirit to teach you to embrace diversity a little more. Then, take a moment to pray for those who have been marginalized or persecuted for their differences.

Close with another hymn or poem which celebrates the diversity in the world, and the joy of finding unity in our diversity.

READING

Revelation 5:1-14

DISCUSSION QUESTIONS

1. What stood out for you in this week's reflections?
2. As you read Revelation 5, identify all the "diversities" that you see there – people, creatures, etc. What does this say about God?
3. How comfortable are you with people and cultures that are very different from your own? How can you become more comfortable?
4. How easily do you greet other people, especially strangers? How can your worship teach you to be a better greeter?
5. How will you live each day with a growing sense of belonging, and how can you help others to feel that they belong, too?

conclusion

where to from here?

*[Christ] existed before anything else, and He holds all creation
together. Christ is also the head of the church, which is His
body. He is the beginning, supreme over all who rise from the
dead. So He is first in everything. For God in all His fullness
was pleased to live in Christ, and through Him God reconciled
everything to Himself. He made peace with everything in
heaven and on earth by means of Christ's blood on the cross.*
– Colossians 1:17-20

LATE FRAGMENT
And did you get what
you wanted from this life even so?
I did.
And what did you want?
To call myself beloved, to feel myself
beloved on the earth.
– Raymond Carver

There are two occasions for which almost all people will
attend a church: weddings and funerals. These two moments,
in which we experience our greatest joy and our greatest grief,
are the times when we most feel the need to connect. Love and
death both confront us with the deepest mysteries of our
human existence. In order to face them effectively, we need to
know that our lives are joined with those of others. We need to
feel that we are not alone in our journey, but that, in the great

scheme of things, our lives matter to God and to others. This is why we come together in rituals that remind us that our journey through this world is common to us all, and yet unique to each one of us.

The sense of having a place in the world need not be reserved for these "extreme" moments. Ideally we should all go through every day knowing that we are at home. It is only this sense of safety and connectedness that can give us the courage to live with open hearts. It is only when we feel that we belong that we can let ourselves really live, and that we can give ourselves to others in ways that help them to be at home as well. This is why we need gatherings and shared rituals that regularly remind us of who we are and what we are here to become. This is why we need to worship.

This book has explored the four practices that together make up the moment of gathering in Christian worship services. It has revealed how the choice to gather opens us to the growth and life of true community. It has shown how the call to worship teaches us to live every moment with a sense of purpose. It has invited us to use the practice of invocation to live with a constant awareness of God's presence and Spirit in our lives and in our world. And it has challenged us to embrace the gift of diversity as we learn to become people of welcome who openly and inclusively greet others in Christ's name. Now it is time to carry the learnings of this journey into the rest of our lives. There are number of ways that we can do this, but I offer only a few here for you to try.

Firstly, I would recommend that, if you're not yet part of a worshipping community, you explore joining one near you. Or, if you are already a regular worshipper, I suggest that you consider renewing or strengthening your commitment to your faith community. *Seek to make the weekly worship gathering a consistent part of your routine.* View it as a spiritual discipline that contributes to your growth and health. As you reflect on your church, try not to measure it by how much the people who attend are like you. Try not to evaluate the worship by how it makes you feel, or by what you get out of it.

Rather, seek to allow your worship to be a place that stretches and teaches you.

Each week, as you gather with others, try to consciously open yourself to the lessons of the liturgy. Ask God to open your heart a little more so that you can risk being connected and vulnerable with your companions in faith. Listen for God's call for the week, and seek to live it out each day. Invite God's Presence to fill and empower you, and try to discern the leading of God's Spirit throughout the week. Finally, make an effort to get to know people who are different from you, and allow their perspectives to inform and expand your view of God, the world, life and yourself.

Secondly, in order to carry the lessons of worship into the rest of your life, you may find it helpful to commit to a *daily personal worship practice.* You may find it helpful to sign up for the Daily Worship devotional guides from my Sacredise website (http:sacredise.com/daily). These short devotions are designed to connect your worship and your life, and to help you to live each day with a conscious sense of following Christ's ways.

Finally, *recognize that living the Jesus way is not something that we learn overnight.* It takes a lifetime to embody the grace, servanthood, justice, peace and love of Christ. It requires time and practice for Christlike actions and attitudes to become the habits that characterize our lives. This means that we need to try, as far as we are able in each moment, to discern how we can reflect the ways of Jesus, and then to act on our best insight. We will often fail and discover that we have thought, spoken or acted in unhelpful or harmful ways. This is part of the learning process. When we recognize our mistakes or sinfulness, we can simply confess, ask for God's forgiveness (and that of the other person if appropriate), and then seek to respond differently next time we face a similar situation. When we choose to live with this constant attitude of learning and growing, we find ourselves changing, slowly but consistently, over time, and little by little our lives come to reflect more of the Jesus way.

I pray that this journey has been helpful for you. If so, please share it with others. Lend them your copy of this book, or buy them one as a gift. Forward the Daily Worship devotionals to them and invite them to join you in worship at your church. For the Reign of God to take hold of our world does not require dramatic movements of vast numbers of people, or miraculous signs in the natural world. All it takes is for each of us to embody the Jesus way in our own lives, and to encourage others to join us in the journey.

My prayer is that each of us will find the courage and the faith to make following Jesus the primary task of our lives, and to embrace worship as the school where we learn how to do it. And that, as we commit to this journey, we will discover that we truly and authentically belong in this world that God loves so much.

John van de Laar
Cape Town

To be notified when the next book in the *Learning to Live* series is available, connect with John online:

Website: Sacredise.com
Daily Worship Website: Sacredise.com/daily
Twitter: www.twitter.com/Sacredise
Facebook: www.facebook.com/DailyWorship

All Sacredise books and CDs can be ordered on the Sacredise website or by sending an email to sales@sacredise.com.

7883496R00079

Printed in Great Britain
by Amazon.co.uk, Ltd.,
Marston Gate.